Hypertext

theory into practice

Edited by
Ray McAleese

EXETER, ENGLAND

Second Edition published in Paperback in Great Britain in 1999 by
Intellect Books
School of Art and Design, Earl Richards Road North, Exeter EX2 6AS, UK

Consulting editor: Masoud Yazdani
Copy editor: Rowena Gelling

British Library Cataloguing in Publication Data available

ISBN 1-871516-28-5

Printed and bound in Great Britain by Cromwell Press, Wiltshire.

Contents

Ray McAleese

Preface: Reflections –
at some time after the event

Early Days . . .

It is now 12 years since this book emerged out of discussions. The discussions
had questions such as: 'Is it worthwhile publishing these papers?', 'Would
anyone read them?', 'Maybe the Chapel Hill Conference will publish some
more useful papers?' These were questions that we did not debate too much:
to those of us who had organised the first UK Hypertext Conference it seemed
that there might be others who would want to read papers. We knew of a
young *and* far-sighted publisher and academic who would give us an
opportunity to have the oral presentations tidied and polished: never let a
good idea escape! So it was that a book of essays emerged from our meeting in
Aberdeen in late 1988.

When I first began *my* journey, that led me to explore the inter-relatedness of
ideas: as a teacher, hypertext was quite unknown to me as a term and was
largely unknown to the academic community and the wider public. I viewed
computer science as an observer, not a participant. I am and was an
educationalist. I stumbled on an idea of hypertext exploding through the
application of computer networks and personal computing.

The gift of hindsight is one that we all possess. The ability to see the
potential of new ideas is one that few can master. I follow the herd and I
marvel at the prescience of Ted Nelson, Jeff Conklin and Vanevar Bush. No
doubt they would speak for themselves: they too might retreat to hindsight.
Nonetheless, whatever the circumstances and no matter how prescient some
might have been, hypertext is the grin of the Cheshire Cat. The cat is long
dead and transmogrified. However, its simple yet tantalising grin permeates
almost every aspect of computing – from home shopping to computer-
supported distance learning, or support groups for the bereaved to interactive
multi-player games.

An Historical Link – for those who really need it . . .

I suppose this section is the 'generalised' footnote. That is, what *hypertext* is
and was – footnotes to distant places, footnotes to associated ideas. Hypertext
was never multimedia. Modality in communication is a totally different

answer to a totally different question: instructional designers use different modalities with multimedia – and abuse them. Hypertext is about the logic of ideas and arguments. Although computer conferencing like CSCW draws on hyperstructures, CSCW is an enabling technology, not an idea in itself. Ideas for CSCW are embedded in social process and the way the workplace resembles a co-operative or competitive cauldron. It is easy to say what hypertext is not.

What *is* hypertext?

I will simply recall some of the applications that were most important to me. Vanevar Bush's 'Memex' is, to most historians, the benchmark. Yet it was the polymath Ted Nelson that gave us the word – well, he 'tells us' he coined the word. I see no reason to doubt him; however, the label or the sign often comes *after* the concept or what is signified. Ted Nelson wanted a unique address for every byte of information in the world – nothing would ever be deleted. Such was his vision. I have in front of me, as I write, an *autographed* copy of *Literary Machines*. Ted Nelson's cover to his own book claims ' . . . this book describes the legendary and daring Project Xanadu, a step on the road toward an instantaneous electronic literature; the most audacious and specific plan for knowledge, freedom and a better world yet to come out of computerdom; the original (and perhaps the ultimate) hypertext system – do not confuse it with any other computer book'. Umm . . . . Not one for under-selling an idea!! It is not surprising that we still really have not seen a workable Xanadu.

It was Andy van Dam at Brown University that developed the first useful hypertext editing system by 1967 – two years after Nelson coined the term. Much later, the Symbolics Document Editor from Janet Walker predated Frank Halaz's seminal work with NoteCards in 1985. It is NoteCards that I hold was the point of take off. NoteCards was pure vision and inspired implementation. It had the browsers and typed links. It gave an integrated operating system, LISP, with an open application layer, NoteCards. NoteCards was both metaphor and implementation for hypertext while it allowed multiple-filing of entitles in separate FileBoxes. Later in time and technology, Brown University developed InterMedia – an underdeveloped system that, like NoteCards, *used* networks of computers with public and private islands of information. This failed, in part, because it was tied to the Apple computer – and it was also a key development. Finally, Ben Shneiderman with HyperTies in 1985 set the seal on the US work. Shneiderman was both human factors guru and prescient information scientist. Each of these innovations gave us at least one ingredient in the US version of hypertext.

In the UK, in 1986, OWL predated Apple's HyperCard with a document editing system. Guide was again an often under-used application. The ideas for using Guide with IDEX – a programmers interface – and with SGML are still fresh today. Back across the Atlantic, the year 1987 provided both Bill

Atkinson's HyperCard and the North Carolina HyperText'87 conference. HyperCard was a key development – and not because of its intuitive interface or because it was on a splendid computer. The Apple HyperCard was key because early versions of it were accessible to any user – it was freely distributed. The public's appetite for hyper-browsing and surfing was fed by early 'stacks' and freely available utilities. Openness is an important element in any innovation.

To me the scene was set. Such stepping stones gave us the bare bones of a causeway to our conference in Aberdeen. So what became of those ideas and the applications? Good ideas persist and applications die – and many should be terminated. It is the Web that inherits the ideas Bush put into his 'Memex' or information organiser. The device that could store all one's books, records and communications. Bush saw the new breed of information managers – his 'trailblazers' – would 'find delight in the task of establishing useful trails through the enormous mass of the common record'. The Internet or the Web is the true descendent of the 'Memex' – the Web Master was born in 1945.

The Web

If there are really some 100 million computers attached to the information web, then it was some of the big ideas of the early hypertext thinkers that has led, in some part, to this explosion. This must be a reason why some still find such early essays as those contained in this book to be of value. The grin of the cat is seen in the impact the Internet is making on education, business and social events. What are the big ideas?

Surfing has replaced browsing. As Hazlitt suggested some two hundred years ago, intellectual travel was – and is – 'a joyous thing'. However, it is the *act* of travelling that is joyous, not the final destination. The association of ideas is as old as writing itself. Philosophers were first to see, or to be aware of, how we as sentient beings link and associate ideas. Surely this must be one of mankind's most identifiable attributes – ripples through ideas connect islands of information. technologies based on the digital computer enabled such ideas to be reified. Without the computer – in particular the connected or networked computer – associationism would have been an interesting but impractical mind-experiment.

Early computer applications treated information like islands. Networking allowed computers to create the nodes or islands that send out and receive the messages from other isolated islands. Servers listened to the requests from clients and passed packets of information in a seemless flow of bytes. Information became related – one island activated another and in turn received an association that gave the traveller new patterns to follow. The ability to stand back and see the linkages as being intentional, vectored and sharing common features gave us, in the wider application-based community, hypertext.

Theory From Practice . . .

In writing this new Preface to a collection of essays on Hypertext and in seeing where Theory emerged from Practice, I would like to share with you, the reader, some of the ideas that generated our parochial interest in this universal phenomena of the nineteen eighties.

First, allow me to make explicit – to exteriorise (as Gordon Pask would have said) the context as I saw it in the early nineteen eighties. I would like to indulge you in one or two reminiscences that are significant in hindsight to me. I want to record the importance of Xerox PARC and its brilliant scientists, some of whom I was privileged to know and associate with – especially Dan Russell and Randy Trigg. I also want to note the importance of some of my work in information science and the seminal work of Blaise Cronin and my friend and colleague Liz Duncan.

As well as ideas and enabling technologies, there were the gritty computer scientists who made things happen at the National Physical Laboratory in Teddington – Bob Watson, Nigel Bevan and David Schofield. These reflections will allow you as reader and observer to see the initial germ of the idea that we stumbled on and that has been taken so far by so many. If only 28 delegates attended the first UK Hypertext 'conference' – I am even hesitant to call it that now – then their ideas have been taken my countless thousands and turned into practice and principles. Let us start a journey by seeing the information world as I encountered it in 1981.

Qualified and Unqualified Associations

One need not rehearse the nature of associationism. It is axiomatic that humans both associate *and* differentiate. We see similarities and we recognise or create differences. In the information world, bibliographic citations provided an important framework for my own work. Being a pedant and an Editor of an academic Journal at the time, I was acutely aware of the way authors create 'generalised footnotes' with citations. This web of citations that Eugene Garfield created with Citation Indexing (just one of his BIG ideas!!) also provided us with a problem. There were too many linkages of the same type. We began with others to question the 'type' of citation made by authors. Was it Evidential, Corroborative, Self-referential, or 'just don't know why – but I need one at this point'!?

Work by Blaise Cronin – then at the British Library, along with my colleague Liz Duncan and supported by the Scottish Education Department – gave us a *qualified* citation index for academic work. Like some good ideas, it was before its time and there were very few implementations (see, however, Unwin & McAleese, 1984 & Chapter 11 for an example in this book). However, the patterns of citing and cited authors with qualified or 'typed' links suggested a powerful metaphor for ideas and navigation through ideas. Enquirers could follow a particular pattern of links though different 'generalised footnotes'. Theses labelled or typed citations also suggested the Concept Map – the cognitive-hypertext. I fell into the educational world of mapping from an information science stance.

The concept map has concept labels associated with other labels in a web of associations. The associations in concept maps are meaningful to learners. A visual or spatial pattern began to emerge. The story of concept mapping is itself interesting, but will have to be told elsewhere. To many in the hypermedia field, the concept map is still a benchmark for a hypertext. My own jump was made when I saw the typed links in the qualified citations. Hypertext had to have links – one link was not necessarily the same as any other link. If citations gave us linkages, it was the technologists and scientists at Xerox PARC that allowed them to blossom. NoteCards was about to 'take-off'.

Browsers and Nodes – Lost in Space

A number of authors have identified the 'Lost in Space' issue. The essay I wrote in 1988 in this volume concentrated on 'browsing': I will comment more on that below. I will also comment on this phenomenon about the essay by Edwards and Hardman. As I see it now, the issue is about having perspective – or better still, the right perspective. Perhaps, having multiple perspectives? Given that any hypertext system could have many thousands of nodes with hundreds of links, even thousands of links, how can the user make sure they keep their goal in focus? Well, the first step is to have a goal. Without some vector, random wandering – what is now called 'surfing' – is inevitable. Even with a goal (e.g. 'to find out if there is a picture of the yeast bacterium that I can use in an essay on fermentation'), there is a vast number of temptations to loose focus. The surfer needs to know 'What is available?'; as well as 'Where is it?' As a modern surfer looks though the search engines, distractions occur that lead to finding out about holidays in the Barossa Valley in South Australia, not pictures of the yeast! A browser should allow the user to see what I have called 'Terrain Knowledge' in addition to 'Street Knowledge'. The 'terrain' is a view of *what is available.* It is ironic that the traveller has often to wander before his or her path is clear. Ambiguity and certainty are happy bed-fellows.

Of course, with only a few nodes, it is simple to show them in one map or diagram. With thousands of nodes new solutions are called for. Fish-eye browsers were a solution that emerged from computer scientists in the 1980s. The fish-eye view – as suggested by its name – gives a very wide perspective with only a few nodes clearly visible in the point of focus. Other nodes are distributed to the periphery of the wide-angle picture. Such devices allow the hypertext navigator to know where they are – Street Knowledge – *and* to see where they might go – the Terrain – before selecting a link. Being lost is sometimes not knowing where to go; it is sometimes not knowing where one has been. Audit trails of links traversed or a generalised 'Undo' operation or a Backtracking function in hypertext allows actions to be reversed and a starting point to be re-found. Commitment is important, but the wise traveller knows when to re-formulate his or her question.

nodes & trails

Typing nodes is another way of clarifying trails. A user can follow one type of link and so limit the number of choices possible. Creating many associations was made possible and with it came the issues of scaling and perspective. The much criticised Alvey Initiative in the UK gave us the impetus to create our own way of managing linkages – with Browsers – and to work with computer scientists from the National Physical Laboratory in separating the structure of the hypertext and its navigation from content at each node.

Authoring and Enabling: designed serendipity

We started to develop Browsers as interfaces to knowledge-based systems in an Alvey collaborative project. The idea was to use the hypertext metaphor along with the Browser interface provided by NoteCards to allow two operations; first to allow experts to give up their expertise, and second, to allow learners to decide what order suited them best. The association with the National Physical Laboratory – producing the first usable hypertext system in the UK, Microtext – was important. We had to interface the navigation and elicitation stages from the delivery stage. By using a network model (it was

network model

possible to implement multi-media on PC-type computers driven by a hypertext system), NoteCards, on Xerox 1186 workstations. User models became the critical stage in the process. It became apparent that somehow we need to anticipate unplanned actions by users!. Designers and excellent computer scientists such as Bob Watson and Nigel Bevan helped us to implement a prototype system. It was the operationalisation of hypertext or hypermedia that the Alvey project enabled. Hypertext systems have to be designed to allow freedom – or at least to support many different actions by different users at different times. Control has to be exercised over choice – without constraining enquiry. Giving a freedom to user to author themselves was a critical step. Users of a complex hypertext system can make their own links and share these with other users. Our debt to the designers of InterMedia at Brown University in this area should be noted.

the context

Three strands came together – the theory of associationism, the need for views and perspective, and the intentional creation of opportunities for users to make their own links. This gave us the context that lead to the essays in this book.

Reflections on the Essays . . .

But what of the individual essays themselves? How do they stand up to the test of time?. As often stated, authors often find it impossible to revisit their own writing after its publication. Often it is because of its torpid style; and often it is because it is just wrong, out of date, replaced by better ideas and needs burial. I have resisted reading most of these essays for at least ten years and I still resist coming to terms with my own ideas. Now it is time to cast caution to the wind and to wonder if there is still something to say about the essays that will help you as a reader to judge them at the end of the millennium that gave us the movable typepress, the marvels of seeing at a distance through television, and the digital algorithmic-computer.

Let us look briefly at each essay. I would like you to use my own questions in the original introduction to preface my comments.

- What questions are the authors answering?

- What can you learn from the authors in their essays?

- Is it possible to corroborate or verify the assertions made?

- Have the authors located the ideas in the appropriate intellectual clearing?

McAleese: Navigation and Browsing
Issue: making the most of mistakes

It is difficult, as I noted above, to be entirely dispassionate about one's own writing. This chapter was largely written after the event and is rather indulgent. There are issues about browsing to consider and there were links to make between the four worlds of computer science, information science, human factors/ergonomics, and education. Looking back, the main issue to stand the test of time is the consideration of navigation as *an intentional activity*. Navigation has to imply a direction – a journey with an endpoint – under most circumstances. The simple view expressed is important as an antidote to 'surfing', yet it is too simple. Failure and serendipity are important elements in learning. as it is *not* always possible to know where one is going to be aware when has got there. The missing element in this chapter is about making the most of events as they occur.

Surfing – or 'wandering' as I called this state in 1988 – is not the most effective strategy – *yet*, great things can come from the unexpected. Learning requires the reflection on experience to precede generalisation. If surfers are aware of their state – surfing – and are not able to recognise useful but unplanned information, they are wandering: that is, lost. The essay I wrote in 1988 is too prescriptive and suggestive that surfing is 'aberrant'. The advanced navigator becomes aware when they are not where they think they are, and then, evaluate the relevance of the situation before moving on. Failure is okay – if one is aware one of failing.

Trigg & Suchmann: Collaborative Writing
Issue: making explicit the tacit to enable sharing and co-operation

Collaboration has itself taken off in the last ten years. In part this is a function of the inter-dependency of computers. In part it is a recognition of the distributed nature of resources and users. The work reported by Trigg and Suchman – key innovators in Xerox PARC and intimately involved with the development of NoteCards – drew on this system's natural open architecture and its distributed nature. I suppose the message that we all have learned about collaborative work is that the technology is easy: the new learning paradigms are more difficult to acquire. Sharing and openness are crucial. Making explicit what it is that one wants to do and keeping records of what has been done give such distributed work added value.

To this has to be added that collaboration has the same tension between focus and surfing. For workers to make the most of the technology there has to be a common purpose; collaboration encourages a vectored approach to tasks. This essay is still fresh and alive. Our office and classroom spaces could be improved with some of Xerox's prescient ideas from many years ago.

Allinson & Hammond: LSE – the Hitch-Hiker's Guide
Issue: travel as a metaphor

Douglas Adams has given us much to enjoy. His often used term – 'Hitchhiker's Guide' – is apt for this essay on Learning Support Environments. The authors tell a spellbinding story of how travel in complex hypertext environments is enhanced by offering multiple routes. The tension referred to above, between vectored travel and multiple opportunities, is well treated for non-formal knowledge domains. I suppose the feature of this essay I still find most useful is its principled approach to learning and navigation. The authors – both psychologists – take a pragmatic view to cognitive processing and offer useful principles. They offer a Hitchhikers Guide – almost a C S Lewis Screwtape Letter from Old Devils to young impudent disciples. They wisely draw general conclusions for the hypertext designer from these principles.

I particularly like their use of the travel metaphor because it resonates with browsing, but 'travel' also because there are different types of transport. Guided tours, go-as-you-please tours, bucketshop there-and-back–only tours, etc. It is important to find a familiar template or metaphor to make sense of hypertext browsing. Some useful ideas are offered in this essay with travel as a metaphor.

Baird & Percival: Database Development using HyperCard
Issue: complexity and accessibility from a non-specialists

I referred above to the emancipatory nature of HyperCard. Pat Baird and Mark Percival make excellent use of this community spirit in designing a *useful* public resource. How many of us have stood outside a city Tourist & Information Office and wondered '. . . where can I get a bed for tonight, and I wonder if there is a nice Indian Restaurant close by, and if I go for Bed and Breakfast, will I be able to get to the station tomorrow morning for the early train . . . ?' HyperCard was well designed for this work. The card metaphor, the layered programming approach, and the ease of tracking, were all attributes to be used effectively.

The authors also tackle the question of complexity. To answer the question I posed above, the hypertext designer needs to afford many routes through the information and ease of error recovery as well as back tracking. This essay also provides very useful evaluation data. While some still use evaluation to sign-off contracts and to please the customer, I sense that the authors really did use formative evaluation to improve their product. I have only one wish. I wish they had said more about reading on small screens and reading lots of information in hypertext environments. Remember the nine-inch screens on Apple SE's that were first used to run HyperCard? I still feel that the users should say '. . . we can't deal with so much information in one chunk. Provide us with more sections and provide some simple organisational structure for the information provided.' We have to face the editing role as hypertext designers. Effective navigation may entail closing off half-open gates and tending to a few broken fences that afford a quick detour.

Cooke & Williams: Design Issues in Large Hypertext Systems
Issue: documents and their structure

I recall this essay as saying important things about reading and accessing technical documentation. The authors used Guide – from OWL – and made effective use of its programming interface, IDEX. I referred above to the under-used nature of Guide. I suspect that the staff from the now defunct Office Workstation Limited would be horrified. However I feel that their application, which came to be used in a kindergarten version and a grown-up version, was not fully appreciated. The delivery metaphor was not simple in comparison with the Note Card or the Hyper Card. Their metaphor was the document.

A document is a complex entity. Its first problem is its inherently linear nature, just like to scrolling Home pages one so often sees on Web sites. Now this idea was not new, but it did allow for some pretty awful designs: not by these authors but by many others who used the simple version of Guide. I still have unused programs written in Guide that are just plain awful to use. The authors of this essay relate an interesting story about the issues in using SGML as an exchange format for complex document sets. The automatic encoding and conversion of disparate document sets is explained here. It reads well after ten years.

Edwards & Hardman: Lost in Hyperspace
Issue: chance and opportunity vs goals

The term 'Lost in Hyperspace' is an icon of the internet age. I have already made reference to it above. The idea signifies the plethora of possibilities that the finite mind of the user has to negotiate when using a hypertext. Like anything that is essentially true, it still has its flaws. Being 'lost' as I suggested above may not be a final state. Learning requires puzzlement and uncertainty. Learning requires the learner to resolve ambiguities and to make sense of the 'senseless'. In learning, experiences are transformed into understanding by the application of conceptual frameworks. Within hypertext it is often difficult to know where one is or has been or where one can go. One must not immediately assume that the unplanned can be predicted or hard-wired. Serendipity – or rather making the most of serendipity – is an attribute of learning.

As I write this Preface, I hear on the radio of a British traveller in Borneo, who was escaping the trials of Western life, being lost for 22 days in the jungle. It seems that he made the most of his opportunities and may even return a more experienced person due to being 'lost'. He may return with a few bites and a few memories of terror, but he may also return with a deeper understanding of first aid and the healing properties of the vines that litter the canopy. Experiences offer learners opportunities to make the most of a situation and *carpe diem* – Seize the Day! One must therefore look with some caution at claims by designers who say being lost is either not possible or undesirable.

Harland: Human Factors Engineering and Interface Development
Issue: planning and control

Before one jumps, one should think what is below. Pre-processing and planning remain essential for the good design of complex knowledge domains. This essay concerns task analysis, system development and human factors engineering as seen in a prototyping activity. One cannot help wonder how much better the current plethora of web pages might be if there was some one thinking: 'what do we add?', 'where shall we add it?' With one Home Page domain, this seems practical: but, like good advice, is often not followed. Within the Internet domain, it is counter cultural. The essence of the Internet, as we have it now, is to allow many flowers to blossom – a veritable Monet's garden. There can be no pre-processing and task analysis that preceeds a new URL or page or panel in a page. The issue the new generation of hypertext designers have to face relate to adopting practices that facilitate users getting to where they want and using the most interesting route possible. Human factors are still an important domain for Internet designers to develop and use.

McKnight, Richardson & Dillon: Authoring of Hypertext Documents
Issue: reading and access to collections of documents

The group from Loughborough provide a very useful and readable account of developing a document taxonomy that aims to assist authors identifying potential links in hypertext documents. This essay has been written by information scientists who are human-factor specialists. They bring their detailed knowledge of documentation and reading to the intentional design of hypertext 'docuverses'. Again continuing the theme developed above, current Internet designers would be well advised to read of the Loughborough experiences and take note of dead links and unconnected nodes. The essay does have some date stamp on it as well as a timeless quality. There were more expectations for the ubiquitous CD-ROM as a delivery mechanism in the 1980s than I see in practice now. CD-ROMs are useful ways of storing and distributing packages of information – 650Mb at a time. Creating a CD-ROM does not in itself create a hypertext. The hypertext is the set of linkages that make available the right information, in the right format, at the right time – Just In Time Information. I would certainly want to see ways of allowing users/learners making their own paths through a complex 'docuverse': delivery is simple, use is an art – or is it a science?

The DHSS Large Demonstrator Project Analysis Tool
Issue: prior analysis leads to more effective implementation

This essay again develops the application theme – that is, creating more accessible electronic documents. This time documents that can be used by the public. Documents that are notoriously difficult to follow – like social security regulations. The Knowledge Analysis Tools developed in this Alvey-supported initiative are really knowledge analysis tools. Graham Stoors notes that the resultant analysis is a bit like creating a semantic net; a net of knowledge nodes linked in a principled fashion to facilitate browsing and structure.

Certainly there are links to be made to the knowledge engineer that one seemed to hear about so much more in the halcyon days of AI developments. The profession – Knowledge Engineer – seemed a desirable label to have on one's passport. I suspect we have emerged from a literal view on this to a more relativist way of thinking about knowledge and what it is. If one accepts – as I hope you might – that knowledge is both transient and asymmetric, then any tools that can make this explicit are useful. Designing a hypertext entails engaging with ideas – thinking about them: it is not, and never was nor can be, simply implementing a computer algorithm. Hypertext is still about ideas: knowledge, whatever that 'commodity' is!

Duncan: Faceted Hypertext
Issue: multiple entities – having ones cake and eating it

My colleague Liz Duncan provides a brief but important insight into the information-scientist's world. In some ways they are divorced from the realities of implementation, but they have – like the experts in any Accessions department in a Library – a clear and sometimes pedantic view on classification. The approach that is adopted by Duncan is most helpful in thinking about hypertext. The use of facet analysis did prove useful in the Alvey project referred to above in the introductory comments. The classificatory process is enabled in the NoteCards 'metaphor', with File Boxes as a virtual holding site for nodes, allowing entities to reside in *multiple cells* of any classification. Facet analysis is *not* an exclusive either/or system; it allows the 'AND' classification. When an entity can be in more than one place, access to it is maximised. Simple classifications (e.g. Dewey) make related books reside in different parts of the Library. Such relatedness may only be in the mind of the reader, but it exists nevertheless. I am not aware how far thinking along these lines has developed over the last ten years: I trust it is making progress.

Kibby & Mayes: Intelligent Hypertext
Issue: anticipation – intelligence in action

The last essay is suggestive of things to come with its use of 'intelligent' hypertext. One wonders, 'is the intelligence in the design, the implementation or the use of the system?' To my very old colleagues, Mike Kibby and Terry Mayes, it had a much less literal meaning. Their real and lasting contribution to thinking about hypertext was to develop a prototype system that used an arcane algorithm to enable links to be computed 'on the fly'. This essay is really about the differences in the hard-wiring of links between nodes (pre-specification) using some model of the user (the 'intelligent approach') and the process of navigation, and travel through information space. They use an interesting framework developed by Hintzman of the Human Memory to suggest a form of node-to-node linking. Computations are not made until a user is in a position to make a choice to move to some other node. StrathTutor was seminal to many as a model for how to develop learning environments. The application was simple but robust and, like some typing tutor developed by Gordon Pask using his Conversation Theory and Lp, seemed to know where the user might most reasonably wish to go next – before the users were aware of it themselves. I will leave the explanation of this mystery to Kibby and Mayes, for StrathTutor and you the reader to consider and investigate.

Enjoy the journey – you never know what you might meet or who you might become as a result of such engagements. Travel well . . . !

Reference
Unwin, D & McAleese, R (1984) *Encyclopaedia of Educational Media, Communications and Technology*, Greenwood Press, Westport, USA. (2nd Edition)

1

Ray McAleese
Overview and questions for readers

Abstract
A brief survey of the chapters in the book and the general themes that emerge.
A number of questions are suggested that readers should bear in mind when
reading the book.

Theme(s)

Fig 1 gives an overview of the papers and their main links indicating issues. The
reader will see from this bird's-eye perspective that there is a wide diversity of
issues, authors and contributing 'knowledge bases'. It is useful to think of a set
of papers as representing the collision of a series of microworlds represented by
the authors. Each author brings to the chapter a whole set of unique knowledge
bases, rule systems and intellectual engines. There is no common pool of
knowledge about hypertext. Indeed, one is sometimes amazed by the lack of
cross-referencing between papers in this field. In addition to the transatlantic
divide which pervades most scholarly writing, there are discipline chasms.
Psychologists, who have a lot to say about mental models and therefore about
hypertext, do not have the same background as Computer Scientists. The reader
should be careful to detect the stance of the authors and realize that like any
neo-natal object, it is yet unset in its true form.

   This figure should also assist the reader to see at a glance the chapter titles, the
relevant page numbers, the links between the chapters and the main topic(s) of
each paper or chapter. A few further words of introduction should help.

   There are two main themes running through the book. First, the metaphorical
nature of hypertext. Researchers agree that it is very important to have an
appropriate way of 'modelling hypertext'. A user's model of the meta-structure
of hypertext not only aids in using any such system, it allows the user (learner,
designer, etc) to have a set of bench marks for hypertext performance.
Definitions such as 'non-sequential browsing' are inadequate without some
metaphor such as a 'journey' to make concrete the users' model of the hypertext
system. User models depend on the ability of the user to realize their intuitive
plans of the system in a series of actions and results. Models without referent

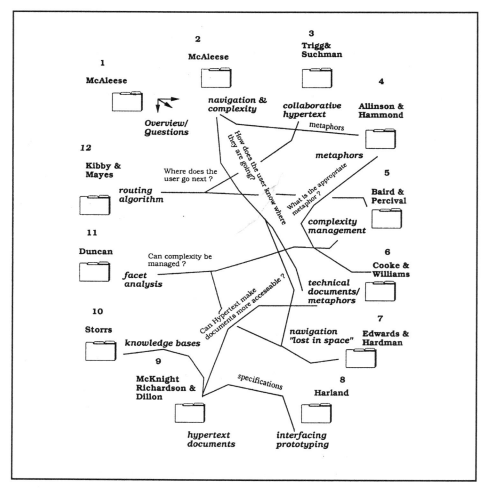

Fig 1 An overview of the papers and their main links

objects or experiences are unlikely to be useful. An analogy is sometimes a more meaningful reference point. However, the analogy requires an isomorphism between the experience or object and the referent experience or object. This is uncommon with computer applications. More useful, perhaps, are the less rigorous conditions of the metaphor where it is sufficient for the user to believe 'it is as if' some object or experience is like some other object or experience. This is what happens when users refer in hypertext to 'notecards', 'journeys', 'browsing', 'windows', 'paths', etc. One cannot underestimate the importance of the metaphor in realizing and facilitating understandings.

Second, the issue of complexity. Hypertext is explosive in its ability to make textual links. Further, hypertext systems, because of their ease of construction, are very rich in text, graphics and visual illustrations. Explosiveness or divergence is common in hypertext. Often it seems that a problem is solved by simply making more and more links between objects until there are no more logical possibilities in order to permit a robust but simplistic user model to be created. It should be obvious that the most efficient or effective way to facilitate a useful system (no matter what its components are) is to improve its precision not its power. Hypertext is a powerful idea. It is not, at present, a precise idea. It is easy to see as a theme the question 'How can hypertext users make such a rich information system manageable?' or 'How can users control access to such systems?'

These are the main themes of the following papers. There is no one starting point (apart from this chapter). The reader should feel free to select appropriate topics or authors. The starting point could be an author's name (Graham Storrs) or a topic (StrathTutor's routing algorithm). In addition, the figure should suggest to the reader a number of links between papers. Five are discernible:

- Where does the user go next?
- How can complexity be managed?
- Can hypertext make documents more accessible?
- What is the appropriate metaphor for hypertext?
- How does the user know where s/he is going?

Each of these links suggests a hypertext link 'where to go to next' if a particular topic/author or paper has been chosen. For example, if the reader chooses to start with Lynda Hardman: Chapter 7, 'Lost in Hyperspace', then a 'good' place to visit next would be Chapter 2, Ray McAleese, Navigation. (Link: how does the user know where he or she is going?) Use this book as a source of ideas. It is after all a HYPERTEXT book. However, be aware of the problems of browsing (see Chapters 2, 7, 9 and 6)!

Questions for readers

In the previous section two themes were identified from the papers as important or central to a study of hypertext. There are of course, a number of other questions that should be addressed by the critical reader. Examining a collection of papers as nodes in a hypertext presents the reader with a hypertext problem of its own: where to start, and where to go next.

The previous section should address this question. To further aid the reader, here are a number of general questions to help navigate through the arguments and information provided.

General questions

1. Consider each paper as the *answer* to one or more questions posed by the author(s). The question may be explicit (how can complexity be managed?), or implicit (what model of the user does the designer have?). Each chapter should make an attempt to answer a question.

Question: What question(s) is the author answering?
2. Each chapter should add a little to the reader's knowledge base of ideas on hypertext. It is unlikely that you, as a reader, will learn nothing. It may be an example, or metaphor or a citation. Look for a message!

Question: What do you as a reader know now that you did not know before you read this paper, section, paragraph?
3. A good argument should stand by itself but should also be able to be validated by the reader's own knowledge. We all know something about hypertext; we may not be able to say exactly what, but something exists. For example, a working knowledge of the travel metaphor, how to use a WIMP interface or experience using a book-based encyclopaedia. However, we should corroborate what any author says with our own experiences in order to fix the ideas for future use.

Question: Is it possible to corroborate the author's assertions in any way?
4. This question leads to a related area of sources and citations. In order to build up any field of knowledge, the information must be accessible - not only to one author, but to many readers. The reader should ask him/herself why the author makes references to others' work. Such hyperlinks are, after all, one of the ingredients of a hypertext system. Ask why the author cites another author at this particular point. If you don't know from the text, then it is unlikely that this will prove a useful path to follow.

Question: Are the authors' citations relevant and accessible?
(see Chapter 11 for a novel and useful way of qualifying citations).

Reference

Hypertext Aberdeen 1988, University Teaching Centre. Papers from the Alvey Human Interface Club, Interactive Learning Systems SIG, University of Aberdeen, ISBN 0 907 258 03 4.

Ray McAleese
Navigation and browsing in hypertext

Abstract

The ability to browse and navigate through hypertext documents is examined along with explanations of the nature of browsing. It is argued that browsing is central to effective hypertext systems and that a variety of tools are required to assist the user make most effective use of the freedom to choose where to go next. Navigation is distinguished from browsing and examples of browsing in NoteCards are given.

Introduction[1]

> *One of the pleasantest things in the world is going on a journey'*
> (William Hazlitt (1778-1830), *On Going a Journey*).

During World War II a poster read 'Is your journey really necessary?'. Few people will actually remember this. However it does remind us, along with Hazlitt, that a journey is both a means and an end. We often use the journey metaphor to characterize our use of information systems. The users' freedom to browse, navigate and take part in a journey or voyage of discovery at will is the most distinguishing feature of hypertext. This chapter is concerned with the way users of hypertext systems exercise that freedom when they browse. Freedom has its costs. Conklin (1987) and others have identified what has become known as the problem of 'getting lost in hyperspace' or 'disorientation'. While this description may be hyperbole, it does give a sense of the importance of browsing and browsing strategies. It also emphasizes the importance of a clear understanding of browsing with regard to hypertext. In addition, it suggests that users new to hypertext will have to adapt to a new set of rules imposed by being able to browse. Freedom to browse may have a concomitant responsibility - the responsibility to ruminate and have strategies. Travel and browsing should not be an effort, unlike the popular aphorism from Robert Louis Stevenson:

> *'to travel hopefully is better than to arrive, and the true success is to labour!'*

What is browsing?[2]

The central notion of a hypertext system is of linking chunks of information together. Akscyn *et al* (1988) make a point that is widely accepted, 'we believe that the ability to browse quickly in a hypermedia system is critical to its usability'. Users of such systems browse or scan or search or trace ideas from one element to another. Further, they expect rapid access to the information required. Information is only a 'mouse movement' away. Users have expectations that when their intellectual window is open on a particular topic they will be able to find out what they do not know 'immediately'. Retrieval of pictures from videodisc has accustomed users to quick information. A typical access time for the laservision player is 2.5 seconds from a database of 50000+ pictures. 'Instant' access to information is important in developing ideas. The ability to follow an idea quickly is an ingredient in browsing.

To follow an idea is to use an 'associationist approach' (Bourne and Restle, 1959). That is, one bit of information triggers an association with another bit of information. One is tempted to equate associationism with modern research theories of parallel processing in neural networks. This temptation should be resisted at this stage! Although associationism is now a discredited psychological explanation of learning, constructivist-cognitive psychologists use some of the associationist's ideas to explain concept-relationship-concept structures (for example see Rummelhart and Norman (1981). Browsing and associationism have a close relationship as we will see below.

Before going further, it is important to note a useful distinction in the use of the terms browsing and navigation with regard to hypertext. There are two states: browsing is where an idea is followed using the linking mechanism of the hypertext elements (eg cards, windows, nodes); navigation involves the use of a graphic aid such as a browser or map to show an overview representation of the nodes and links. This distinction has not always been made. Hammond and Allinson (1988) use the term navigation to refer to browsing (with the system in control) and browsing with the learner in control. The distinction made above will be developed later when aids to browsing are discussed.

Let us begin by looking at browsing from a traditional information retrieval point of view. Readers who are users of information systems are familiar with the general idea of browsing along library shelves. Let us see what this activity consists of from an information retrieval standpoint. The reader might require to check up some details of an idea in a familiar book that is not available in their office or study, for example, an item from the list in Shneiderman's Researcher's Agenda for Menu Selection Techniques. Let us assume that the reader knows the title and the author of this book, 'Designing the User Interface' by Ben Shneiderman, but does not know the exact chapter or page in this work. Indeed, the searcher has forgotten what exactly Shneiderman said! The reader might go straight to a library to look for the particular item of information (eg 3rd Floor Queen Mother Library, 2nd Room , 4th Shelf, Chapter, Page, in Aberdeen). If they know the exact location, then the book can be retrieved assuming no one else is using it!

If the exact location of the book is not known then a classification system is normally used (Dewey, UDI, etc) to assign a standard code to the item. This code will give a unique address to the book (178.234). Items with common codes tend to be stored together by libraries. With this information the reader can go purposefully to the relevant shelf in the relevant part of the library. An author or subject index is used to guide the reader within the book. While the reader is at the appropriate shelf location (or page), other items are often noticed. This is particularly important when the 'target' item is not found, or when the idea being sought is not clear. Readers will find themselves beginning to look along shelves, dipping into different books, looking up tables of contents and indexes. Such distractions are interesting, but they may not be purposeful. It is rather like the distractions provided by the display of items in shop windows when the reader is walking along a shopping street. Likewise with pages and paragraphs in a book - or ideas in an argument.

The information-seeking activity described above is the simplest form of information browsing. Browsing is using associations (or links) to determine the next item to be accessed. Such associations can be either explicit or implicit.

Many other examples will come to mind such as reading the newspaper in the morning. The reader will 'scan' the pages using the headlines to indicate if something is worth reading in detail. The reader's eye will cover the pages in a wide variety of ways depending, in part, on the typographical cueing used. It is interesting that many readers, when they 'scan' a newspaper, do so in reverse order of pages. While this has more to do with the way the sheets of the paper are folded, it indicates that a logical sequence or layout for any particular reader is neither linear nor west European - ie top to bottom, left to right. Browsing, and its related ideas (navigation, scanning, etc), are familiar and yet require being made explicit in order to make the most of their potential.

It is important to begin with browsing as seen by information scientists. Although text browsing is often specific and constrained by the context (books, journal articles, etc), it is a useful benchmark for a more precise definition within hypertext. A number of sources are worth consulting: Salton (1971), Palay and Fox (1981) and Morse (1973) are good starting points. Hildreth (1982) is an excellent survey. Batley (1989) and to a lesser extent Foss (1987) are most relevant to hypertext.

Morse (1973) describes browsing as:

> *'a type of search... by an observer in a plane, for an enemy ship or submarine on the ocean surface.... The observer is not sure where the target is... but he flies a search pattern in hope of success'*

Two points can be drawn from Morse. First, browsing is seeking for new information and second, there is at least one type of browsing where the information sought is unknown but anticipated. Meadow (1973) indicates the goal-directed nature of browsing information:

> 'We enter this process with a general idea of the subject of the search ..... with a few very specific descriptors - perhaps a title or author'

Hildreth (1982) suggests a more random element in browsing:

> '.. the most visible and commonly understood browsing activity is roaming among the shelf areas of a Library or Bookstore...'

Roaming suggests the serendipitous nature of some types of browsing. However, Hildreth (1982) does not leave browsing without allowing for more purposeful activity:

> '... browsing is frequently a purposeful activity occasioned by a felt information need or interest'.

However Batley (1989) points out :

> 'The purpose of the activity (browsing) is not so much to explore but to find.'

She goes on to make an important distinction between browsing and non-browsing. Browsing is 'exploratory, vague, non-specific and has associated activities of exploring, scanning and extending'. While non-browsing is 'exclusive, specific and has associated the activities of getting, focusing and narrowing'. Browsing, she claims, is more purposeful and focused. It is more concerned with having a model of what might be possible and exploring options to see which meets implicit criteria. Indeed the purpose of browsing may be quite implicit or tacit in the understanding of the searcher, yet the need for information is there.

Types of browsing

There are, of course, different types of browsing. O'Connor (1985) describes three types of browsing: systematic, purposeful and serendipitous. In his analysis he concentrates on the purpose or perceived purpose of browsing as seen by the user. This is corroborated by Apted (1971) who contrasts Specific Browsing where 'the user has some knowledge of the intended direction of his search which is not casual or haphazard' and General Purposeful as 'discovering unspecified but useful information'. Batley points out this distinction between specific and purposeful. She defines them as follows:

> 'Specific: where the user searches for information within certain parameters; Purposeful: more exploratory process....where the user searches for information without creating boundaries within which to concentrate effort.'

While these points sharpen up the way information scientists see browsing, it is Oddy (1977) who helps us with hypertext systems. He suggests that browsing can be:

'facilitated in a deliberate way by arranging information in a way within which exploration can take place'

Returning to Hildreth, he makes the claim that it is structure imposed upon information that facilitates browsing. His claim highlights the importance of summaries and indexes to give a bird's-eye view of the content. Without this overview, it is argued, it is difficult to achieve purposeful browsing. Such overviews can be thought of as being useful for navigation. Morse (1973) comes closest to defining a browsing session in a hypertext system when he emphasizes the need to differentiate between the 'interest potential' of information chunks. In order to distinguish one element from another he suggests it is important to provide some form of information- or relevance-cueing. Structure, also emphasized by Conklin (1987), and cueing are important in order to facilitate effective browsing. Monk *et al* (1988) agree with this conclusion after examining a variety of presentation methods in hypertext in a series of experimental studies. They say:

'...hypertext provides exciting new ways of structuring information, but it should be remembered that there are already well understood ways for communicating non-linear conceptual structures in conventional linear text'

It should, therefore, be remembered that users of hypertext systems bring to their task old ideas that may be of considerable use, for example, typographical cueing such as headings, font size, type and width etc (Stewart, 1987).

Browsing strategies

Different authors write of browsing 'strategies' in different ways. For example, some refer to 'browsing operations' when they mean preprocessing operations before 'scanning' or 'browsing' takes place. Larson, 1986 suggests four basic browsing operations: structuring, filtering, planning and zooming. Structuring is where someone preprocesses the information to facilitate browsing by a user. Filtering selects out relevant information for a client. Planning is equated with navigation or scrolling through information. Zooming determines the detail of the information displayed. Such preprocessing activities are important in providing most usable information in terms of access.

A study of the way users of a database approached browsing by Canter *et al* (1985) provides us with the most useful parallells for hypertext. The research concerned the way users navigated through a database. They devised a series of indices for the paths chosen: pathiness, ringiness, loopiness, spikiness, number of nodes traversed, and the ratio of the number of different nodes visited to the number of visits to nodes. Using these indices they conclude that there are five discernible search strategies:

'Scanning: covering a large area without depth.

Browsing: following a path until a goal is achieved.

Searching: striving to find an explicit goal.

Exploring: finding out the extent of the information given.

Wandering: purposeless and unstructured globe trotting.'
(Pask and Scott, 1972)

Each of these strategies, except for the last, has an appropriate place in hypertext. Scanning and exploring are used to get an overview of an application. Browsing is following a train of thought and searching is following an idea to a leaf node or to a dead end. One can apply these strategies in a number of ways. For example, applying them to different types of browsing interfaces. There are two main types of interface: Type 1, the card or frame with 'hot spots' or 'active icons'; Type 2, the graphical interface consisting of node - link - node representations of the extent of the hypertext system. The five-fold classification referred to above indicates different patterns of use when Type 1 and Type 2 interfaces are compared.[3]

	Street View	Terrain View
	Type 1 Interface	**Type 2 Interface**
	Textual	Graphical
Scanning	**	**
Browsing	***	*
Searching	**	*
Exploring	*	**
Wandering	*	***

*	Some tendency to use
**	A tendency to use
***	Very high tendency to use

Table 1 *Comparison of Type 1 and Type 2 Interfaces*

It can be seen from Table 1 that there is a tendency for the graphical interface (Type 2) to encourage users to seek the extent of the knowledge/information and produce unstructured journeys whereas Type 1 interfaces are more likely to

Strategy	Description	Representation
Scanning	A mixture of deep spikes and short loops as users seek to cover a large area but without great depth. High NV/NT. High SQ. Medium LQ.	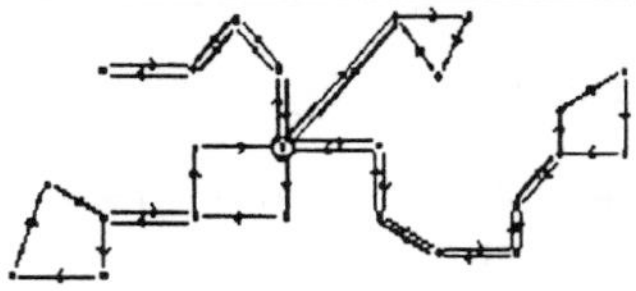
Browsing	Many long loops and a few large rings, where users are happy to go wherever the data takes them until their interest is caught. Medium LQ. Medium RQ. Medium NV/NS.	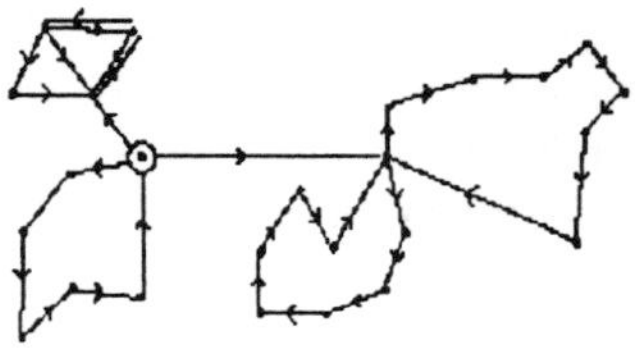
Searching	Ever-increasing spikes with a few loops for users motivated to find a particular target. High SQ. Medium LQ. Low NV/NS.	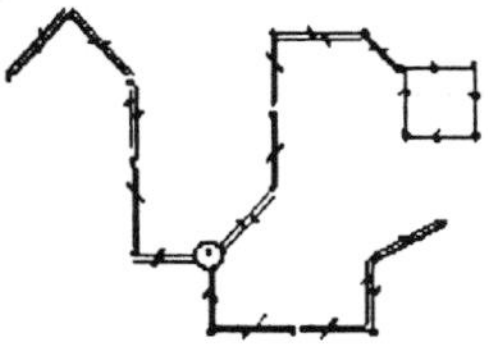
Exploring	Many different paths, suggesting users who are seeking the extent and nature of the field. High PQ. High NV/NT.	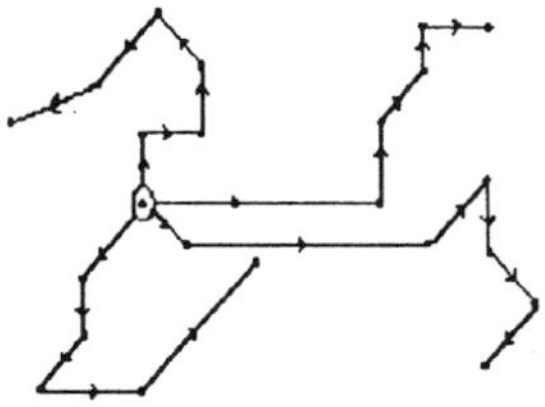
Wandering	Many medium-sized rings as the user ambles along and inevitably revisits nodes in an unstructured journey. High RQ. Low NV/NS. Medium NV/NT.	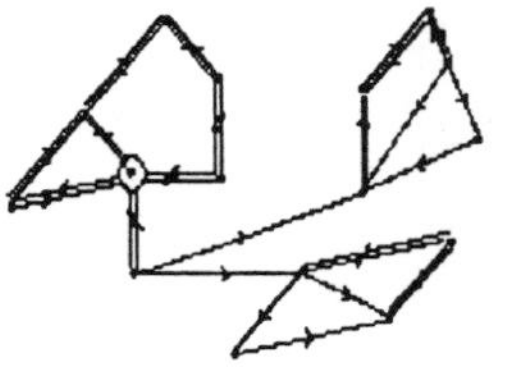

Table 3 : Search strategies.

[⊙ = Starting Point or 'First Page']

Fig 1 *Browsing strategies (from Canter et al)*

produce browsing and scanning, where users are happy to go wherever the links suggest until an end point is found.

Strategies such as those identified by Canter *et al* are patterns of acquired behaviour used by the searchers to achieve their goals (implicit or explicit). Such strategies need not be explicit. Strategies can be learned.

Hierarchical structures

The net metaphor used to understand the links between elements inhypertext is very often misunderstood. Taken literally a net implies that no one node is 'more important' or 'central' than any other node. In a true network system any node should be assessable at one link distance from any other node. Often there are constraints placed on this ideal solution in order to minimize the number of links held. A constrained net with a limited set of links is most frequently found in hypertext. A fishing net is a better metaphor and permits hierarchies to be imagined. Imagine a fishing net with knots for nodes. Every node has links to several other nodes, usually three or four. Browsing using such a network is constrained. Access is not to any of the N-1 other nodes (where N is the total number of nodes) but to any 3 or 4 other nodes. Further, and most important, imagine one can pick up any node. Other nodes fall about this central or 'top' node in a cascade. One node (the one selected) is at the apex of a hierarchy of nodes. Such structuring is important in providing the browser with scaffolding to support purposeful browsing.

Hypertext, as well as providing the freedom to get lost, can use hierarchical structuring to provide the supports for the user to achieve desired goals. By providing an 'ideational scaffolding' (Ausubel, 1974) with a small set of link types, a user's expectations can be confined and become more educative. That is, the user begins to acquire the same scaffolding for his own ideas. Often the implicit structure of the hypertext system gives the user support. For example, NoteCards uses a hierarchical structure in its use of File Boxes, (see also Halasz *et al* (1987) for details of NoteCards).

Browsing and hypermedia

Browsing takes on a new dimension when the elements through which the users move are pictures (static and dynamic) and perhaps objects (virtual and real). Batley (1989) has examined the way pictorial information can be retrieved from 'visual databases'. Extensions of traditional hyperTEXT systems to encompass hyperMEDIA introduces a new dimension. Batley identifies a problem for hypermedia systems. With the introduction of pictorial information the ability of the user to impose structure and express intent or purpose is made more difficult by the very visual nature of information. Pictures are, of course, very different from text or graphics in the amount of information they contain. A black and white picture made up of a horizontal resolution of 1200 pixels and a vertical resolution of 900 pixels with no grey scale contains 1.08 mega bits of information. An A4 page with 70 characters per line and 60 lines per page contains 4.2 kilo bits of information. The 260-fold difference is mirrored in the degree of ambiguity that can be seen in a high resolution colour picture. This ambiguity is at the root of the problem with regard to browsing. The picture that 'speaks a thousand words' may say a thousand different words to different viewers. Pictures or graphics lend themselves much more than does text to multiple interpretations. Indeed, it is this ability of the picture to allow different interpretations that provides its richness as an educational stimulus. Multiple goals and multiple paths to those goals are facilitated by picture-based hypermedia systems.

Browsing tools

Given that there are problems with browsing, are there any solutions? Carolyn Foss (1987) , in exploring ways to avoid getting lost, describes two phenomena she calls the 'Embedded Digression Problem' and the 'Art Museum Problem'. In the former, the user keeps following chains of thought until the original goal is lost, a common problem in using an encyclopaedia with cross-referencing. Try the term {Sonata} in the Encyclopaedia Britannica! The Art Museum Problem is the situation where, after spending a long period browsing through many images, there is a loss of distinction between the individual items and an inability to abstract the general characteristics from the particular. Foss observes:

> 'Forming a coherent understanding or abstraction of what you have viewed is important for effective browsing'.

Foss evaluated two solutions with regard to NoteCards and the use of unconstrained versus filtered browsers (showing only specified links). To combat the problems she developed two types of aid, the Graphical History List and The History Tree. The Graphical History Lists records and displays every neighbourhood of nodes a user has examined in a session. Cards (i.e. nodes) are marked and the user can easily see which links have been followed. History Trees record exactly the cards (nodes) that have been accessed and display a hierarchical list of the user's trail. A special case of the History Tree is further described as the Summary Tree where a user's historical path through a network is displayed with annotations made by the user. Foss's tools are similar to those suggested in this context by Weyer (1982) with respect to a dynamic book. In his system every article in the 'encyclopaedia' contained a sublist with names of articles referenced to it. With regard to the graphical display Foss makes an important contribution to an understanding of browsing. (NoteCards, because of its extensibility (Halasz,1987) is particularly helpful in this regard.) Another tool is provided in HyperCard.

HyperCard provides a useful facility with the Summary window called by the 'Recent' command. This command allows the user to see up to 42 of the most recent cards visited. In effect the nodes viewed, as shown below, were not in a particular sequence, but were the last nodes visited in the stack (the last unique cards). This graphic summary tool meets some of the requirements made by Foss in her History List NoteCard-type. Fig 2 shows the HyperCard overview.

Tools that help the user see where they have been (history) have been developed by other hypertext system designers. For example, SemNet Fisher *et al* (1987) has a

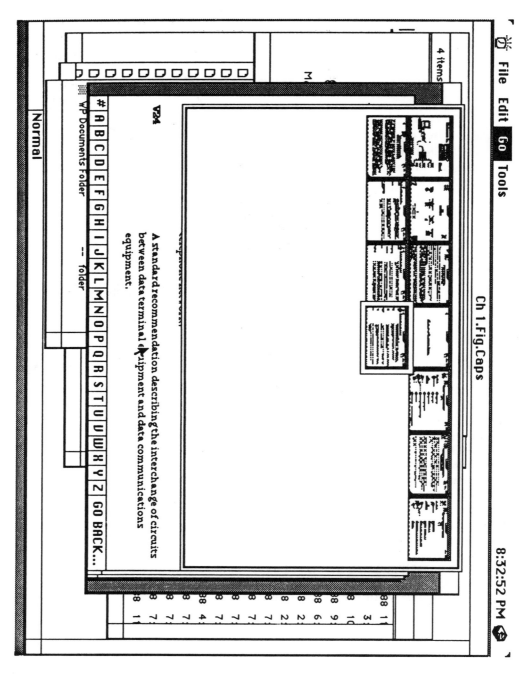

Fig 2 *HyperCard overview*

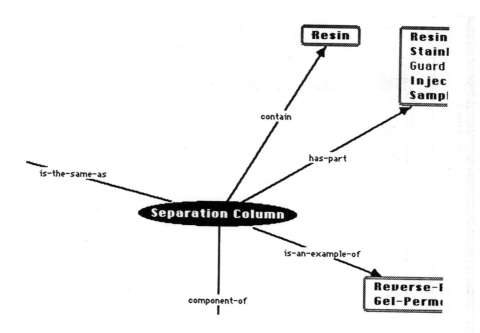

1: open at.........Separation Technique
2: ---is-used-for-->HPLC
3: ---comprises-->Recorder
4: ---component-of-->HPLC
5: ---comprises-->High Pressure Pumps
6: ---component-of-->HPLC
7: ---comprises-->Separation Column
8: ---has-part-->Injector
9: ---changes-->Switch
10: ---changes-->Injector
11: ---passes-sample-to-->Column
12: ---is-the-same-as-->Separation Column
13: ---is-an-example-of-->Reverse-Phase
14: ---type-of-->Resin
15: ---contained-by-->Stainless Steel Col.

Fig 3 *SemNet history*

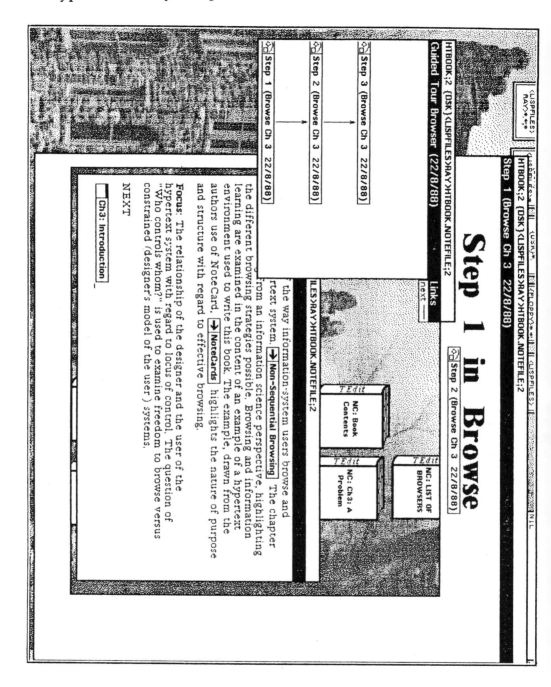

Fig 4 *Table-top guided tour, step 1*

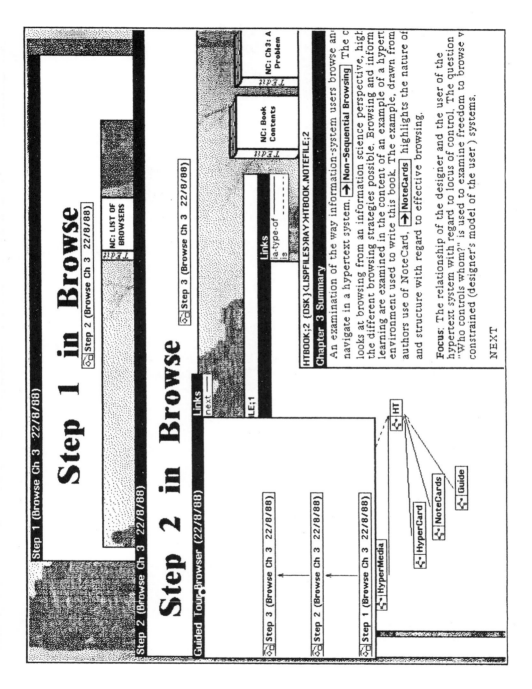

Fig 5 *Table-top guided tour, step 2*

backtrack path facility which shows in a linear list the nodes visited and the link types used (see Fig 2). In this example, the user was browsing a knowledge base on HPLC techniques (in molecular biochemistry). He started at the node {HPLC} jumped to the node {Separation Technique} using the [is-used-for] link-type. From the {Separation Technique} node he jumped to the {HPLC} node again and from there to {Detection System} using the [comprises] link and so on. The tool displays the nodes and links that have been visited. In addition, whilst using the path, any node in the list can be selected and a jump made back to that point.

Similarly, StrathTutor in Chapter12 permits the learner to see a backtrack of the frames visited. This 'history' tool can be used by the learner to answer the questions 'Where have I been?' or 'What do I or should I know?'. The system designer or tutor can use this trace facility to analyse the routing made by groups of students through instruction.

See also Chapter 3, *Collaborative Writing in NoteCards* for another example of a 'History Card'.

Many other examples of 'trails' exist. For example, Vannevar Bush (1945) spoke of a series of trails through his 'memex'.

> '... when numerous items have been joined together to form a trail, they can be retrieved in turn, rapidly or slowly...'

Trigg and Weiser (1986) used trails in their Textnet system. Here the path, as they call it, could be saved, named and used as an entity itself. Hammond and Allinson (1988) use a similar approach in their guided tour. Scripts may also be used to connect elements in multimedia documents. These scripts form electronic threads or trails.

Mylonos (1988) has extended HyperCard scripting to give a tour facility. A 'next' button can access a sequence of frames using an appropriate script that computes the next card to bring up.

Trigg and Weiser (1988) using NoteCards gives examples of two tools. The Table Top card is a way of capturing the layout of a set of NoteCards on the screen. A Table Top is a snapshot which includes all the details of the cards in order to reconstruct a snap at a later point. When constructing such a Table Top, the user selects which elements go into the snap. Once selected, the user has access to an historical snap at any time. The Guided Tour facility consists of a graphic interface between Table Tops. Trigg and Weiser (1988) describe the Guided Tour as:

> 'a graph where nodes are Table Top cards and where edges are Guided Tour links connecting the cards. '

Once the tour is set up, a subsequent user (or the original user at another time) can replay the tour using a simple set of commands (eg Start, Jump).

Figs 3 and 4 show an example of this technique which the present author used in tracing steps in browsing. The task here relates to writing a textbook on hypertext! The nodes in the graph are snaps of the states of the screen during a browsing session.

In Fig 4 the graphical interface [Guided Tour Browser (22/8/88)] can be seen with one of the nodes displayed [Step 1 Browse Chapter 3 22/8/88)]. In Fig 5 the second node has been displayed. Each of the steps in the browser can be represented by a node which itself can be displayed. Paths used in this way are a useful evaluative tool for hypertext interface design as well as demonstrators. The examples above are static in comparison to Trigg and Weiser (1988). In his example, each of the sub-elements in the Table Tops (snaps above) can be activated (see *Collaborative Writing in NoteCards*, Chapter 3).

Browsing and learning

One of the aims of hypertext is to enhance existing learning strategies. Learning by exploration is one of the most powerful strategies for certain types of information and certain learning goals. Exploring in this way is occasioned by known concepts triggering off new ideas or by the learner attempting to make a link between two previously known ideas. In hypertext this has its parallel with a node triggering another node and a learner or designer making a link or association between existing nodes. A discovery approach is a situation where what is to be learned is determined independently by the learner. Guided discovery places the locus of control in the hands of the teacher or teaching materials. Learning, while it is not without its definitional ambiguities, is seen as being concerned with linking, relating, structuring, restructuring, adding, collecting, and adapting. Ideas that have been learned can be called knowledge. Knowledge that exists (concepts, principles, images, networks, etc) is changed by an active process of knowledge seeking. Without active intentions and motivation effective learning will not take place. Creating this active atmosphere is what hypertext systems can do. The activity of using a hypertext system must be directed as opposed to random. It is not effort itself that delivers success, but vectored or directed activity.

There are other aspects to learning to be considered. Learning takes place at a meta-level as well. Not only learning concepts as such, but learning what is known, how many concepts are mastered and what they are, also what is unknown (McAleese 1986). Central to meta-cognition is the need to express a felt information need. Based on the way information scientists see information seeking, browsing is an effective way of negotiating implicit goals. It is often said that making explicit the implicit is the hardest part of effective information seeking. Rhode (1986) emphasizes the necessity of making information needs explicit:

> ' *information need is seen as a subjective relative concept existing only in the mind of the experiencing individual*'.

He goes on to identify 'unfelt' needs as the most difficult category of information - the need to understand. Sometimes searchers know what they know, sometimes they can only come to know by exploring, seeking and using different structuring strategies to help them give up their goals. This is quite a common phenomenon in information retrieval. Belkin and Vickery (1985) suggest that the information seeker is essentially engaged in a 'problem solving activity':

> 'a person with some problem or goal decides that his or her state of knowledge is insufficient or inadequate for accomplishing a goal. He or she therefore has recourse to some knowledge resource... The person's access to this resource is through an intermediary mechanism whose role is to help the user obtain an appropriate response...'

Ingwersen (1986) provides the closest description of the hypertext problem when he says:

> 'each single step in the information retrieval process for the individuals involved, is concerned with problem solving and learning situations'.

Browsing and navigation are concerned with discovery. For learners, they begin to know better where they want to go and, as a result, what they know and don't know.

An example

In order to highlight the nature of the browsing issues and to suggest some solutions and examine some tools let us look at a hypermedia system used by the present author. This example deals only with the NoteCards applications.[4] The hypertext system requires a number of NoteCards files. Seven are used extensively, although several others are used from time to time. The files are:

HTBOOK: the main hypertext 'chapters' and 'sections' of this book. This file also controls the hypertext version of the book.

HTBASE: a knowledge base of concepts used. HTBASE uses a limited set of thirteen semantic link types based on Aberdeen research in constructing an intelligent interactive video system in an Alvey project (MMI 110).

HTBIB: a hypertext bibliography which allows the author to control the retrieval of sources from books, journals, etc.

HTIDEAS: a file that was used to be a scratch pad of hypertext ideas as they arose.

CASP: a hypertext tutorial file which described the Aberdeen research in knowledge and information mapping (KIM).

NEWIDEAS: a general scratch file which the author used to note down and link ideas relating to computers and computer applications in information use.

THES: a thesaurus of terms used to provide a 'knowledge base' of links between keyword terms assigned to the bibliographical records. THES is a way of linking disparate bibliographical records or hypertext elements using a knowledge base of terms with only Broad Term (BT), Related Term (RT) and Narrow Term (NT).

Although each NoteCards file is independent, each can be linked to another; that is, the complete file containing the chapters of the book (HTBOOK) can be linked to the file containing the knowledge base of terms used - HTBASE (Global to Global links). Further, each element in any notefile can be linked to any other element (an element is a chunk of hypertext or graphics or picture); that is, a single bibliographic record can be linked in one file to a section in a chapter in another file. Likewise a thesaural term can be pointed to by a bibliographic record or a chunk of text and vice versa (Specific to Specific links).

Suffice to say, a NoteCards file consists of text, graphics and/or 'browsers'. Each of these elements can be operated on using an appropriate editor. Links between different nodes are indicated in the 'cards' by icons. Selecting an icon will expand the node represented by that icon (see Halasz *et al* 1987; Irish and Trigg 1989).

The most important point to remember here is that NoteCards permits multiple windows showing multiple information elements concurrently. Unlike HyperCard, and other Hypertext systems, NoteCards allows many information items to be concurrently accessed. See also Chapter 3, Collaborative Writing in NoteCards.

Fig 6 shows a screen on a Xerox 1186 workstation that arose during a typical authoring session. Figs 7 to 12 show some of the general problems associated with a free unconstrained browsing system. An example is taken in Figs 7 to 12 which follows the author's 'train of thought' through a series of nodes.

In the construction of a hypertext or hypermedia system there are a number of authoring strategies. These are:

capture, expansion, linking, sequencing [5]

The example in Figs 7 to 12 shows the author in a Linking mode.

To begin with, let us look at some of the basic background. Fig 6 shows a typical desktop from the NoteCards system.

Reading this figure clockwise from the top left corner the reader will be able to see a complex information problem. On top of the desktop (a picture in this case) the author has a number of active editors or tools. The filing box icon is the NoteCards top level menu. From this, macro functions are executed. The 'CHAT' icon is a shrunken window from a terminal emulator. This gives teletype and file transfer over an RS232 line. The next five icons represent file browser tools from the InterLisp operating system. The window at the top right is the first NoteCards window to note. This represents the top level of the bibliography file. Here it is an alphabetical list of authors. Immediately below this is the first piece of textual hypertext, an example taken from the CASP file. Bottom right is a rough note from the HTIDEAS file about a new development reported on a Macintosh Bulletin

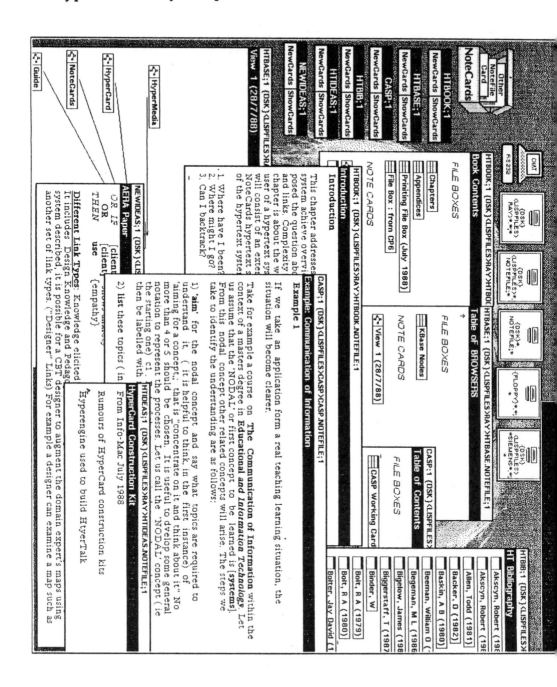

Fig 6 *Typical desk top screen during authoring.*

Fig 7 *Tidy desk top at start of browse.*

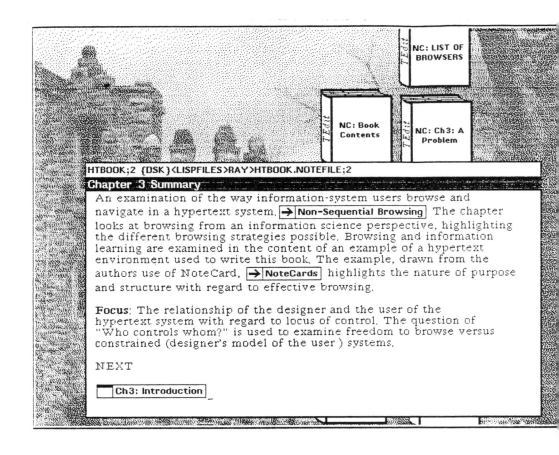

Fig 8 *Initial card with an idea for a summary.*

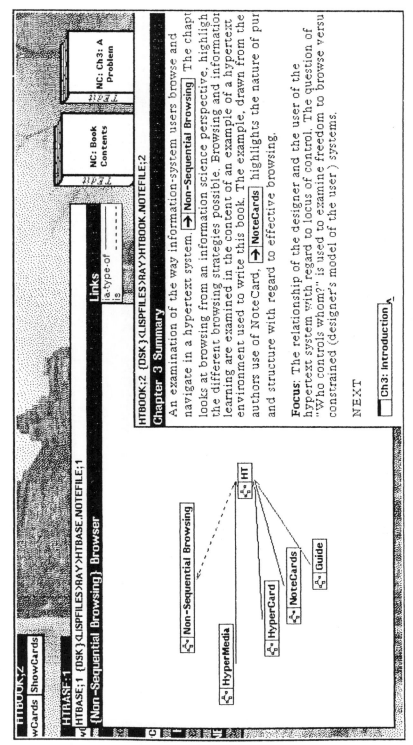

Fig 9 *Summary card along with an overview*

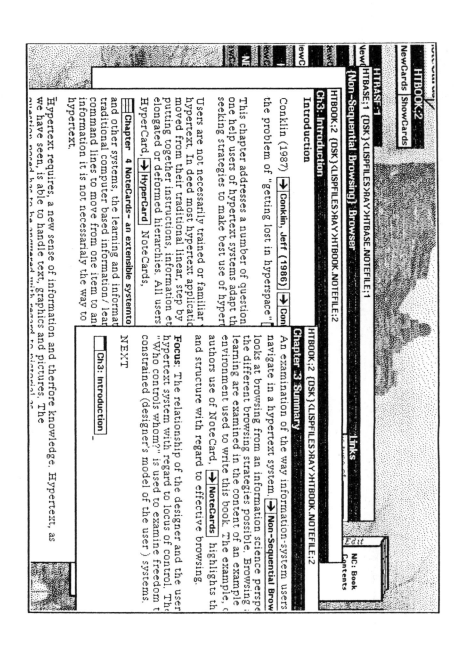

Fig 10 *Summary card, with introduction and embedded link icons.*

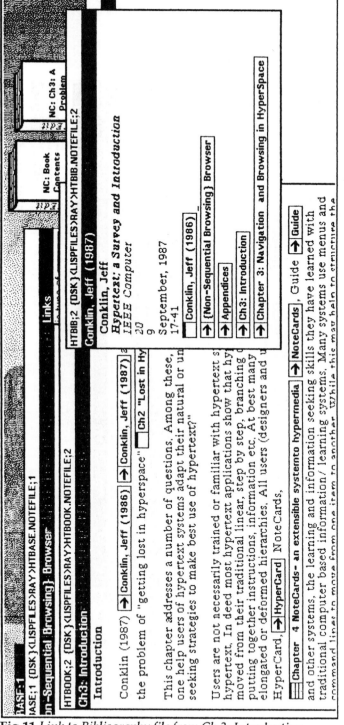

Fig 11 *Link to Bibliography file from Ch 3: Introduction.*

28

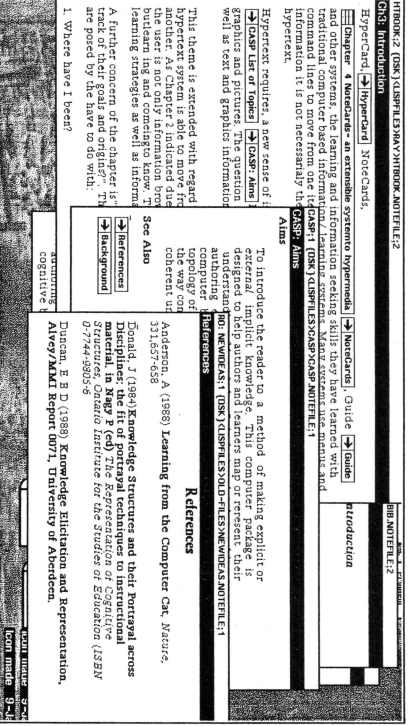

HTBOOK;2 {DSK}<LISPFILES>RAY>HTBOOK.NOTEFILE;2

Ch3: Introduction

Chapter 4 NoteCards– an extensible system to hypermedia, NoteCards,

HyperCard, HyperCard, NoteCards, Guide Guide

and other systems, the learning and information seeking skills they have learned with
traditional computer based information/learning systems. Many systems use menus and
command lines to move from one item... **CASP;1 {DSK}<LISPFILES>CASP>CASP.NOTEFILE;1**
information it is not necessarily the... hypertext.

CASP: Aims

Hypertext requires, a new sense of i...

CASP List of Topics CASP: Aims

graphics and pictures. The question...
well as text and graphics information

CASP: Aims

Aims

To introduce the reader to a method of making explicit or
external implicit knowledge. This computer package is
designed to help authors and learners map or represent their
understand...

This theme is extended with regard...
hypertext system is able to move fro...
another. As Chapter 2 indicated due...
the user is not only information bro...
but learning and coming to know. T...
learning strategies as well as inform...

authoring...
computer...
topology of...
the way con...
coherent u...

RO: NEWIDEAS;1 {DSK}<LISPFILES>OLD-FILES>NEWIDEAS.NOTEFILE;1

References

A further concern of the chapter is...
track of their goals and origins?". Th...
are posed by the have to do with:

See Also

References
Background

1. Where have I been?

Anderson, A (1988) **Learning from the Computer Cat**, *Nature*,
331,657-658

Donald, J (1984) **Knowledge Structures and their Portrayal across
Disciplines: the fit of portrayal techniques to instructional
material, in Nagy P (ed)** *The Representation of Cognitive
Structures, Ontario Institute for the Studies of Education (ISBN
0-7744-9805-6*

Duncan, E B D (1988) **Knowledge Elicitation and Representation,
Alvey/MMI Report 0071, University of Aberdeen.**

introduction

BIB.NOTEFILE;2

Fig 12 *Three linked files*

Board (MacTel). Along the bottom, and partly hidden, is a part of a description of link types from an AERA paper that is in the NEWIDEAS file. Hidden at the bottom and the left is a browser or graphical display of a knowledge base.

This base uses the NoteCards nodes to represent concepts relevant to writing the book at the time the 'snap' was made. Tools and layout change over time and with particular tasks. Each of the windows, representing text items, browsers or graphics, can be accessed for editing by the user by pointing at it. The stage of the authoring process at which the window was 'snapped' was Linking. That is, the author having created some information and expanded it or developed it in isolation, is making links between the different elements in this case for the user (learner). The ability to access any selected item or window places the user in control.

No overriding model of the task or the user is controlling the way the user accesses the windows. It should be obvious that not only is there complete user control, but any system would be unable to determine which window is 'active' given that the user can read non-overlapping items. This freedom places this particular hypertext system in a special category. This Figure shows the degree of freedom given a user by the NoteCards system. Freedom, of course, has its concomitant aspect - responsibility. Here responsibility means the responsibility to maintain a tidy desk top!

Figs 7 to 12 show a browse or a train of thought using the available NoteCard files.

Fig 7 starts with a tidy desk top showing three open NoteCard files (HTBOOK, HTBASE and HTBIB). A number of hypertext elements have been shrunk to icons and appearing on the right of the Figure (eg NoteCard 'Chapter 3 Summary' - top left of the icons). The author started by opening up the element 'Chapter 3 Summary'. This shows in Fig 8 a few lines of text with three NoteCard Link Icons. The author selected the icon [Non-Sequential Browsing] which produced the graphical display seen in Fig 9. From the 'Chapter 3 Summary' the author selected the item labelled 'Ch3: Introduction'. This has appeared in Fig 10. In Fig 11 the author moved to the bibliographic reference, Conklin (1987). Returning to 'Ch3: Introduction' the author moved further down this element until the icon 'CASP : Aims' was selected. Fig 12 shows this node and the next in line (the seventh since the start of the browse), a Reference element from the CASP NoteCard. Starting with a summary of a chapter, the author, through a series of steps, has moved to another area with pointers to further areas in the Reference List. Table 2 overleaf takes each of these steps and, using the author's own notes made at the time, reconstructs a 'train of thought' through the nodes. Remember, the author is examining the hypertext system in order to build a tutoring/learning system.

Step	Commentary
1	Start with the Summary for this Chapter.
2	What other concepts are related to Non-Sequential Browsing? No link here.
3	Move on to the Introduction. Link here: Summary to Introduction.
4	Conklin should be central to the arguments about browsing, I wonder where else he has been referred to? Link here: provide link to Conklin to allow user to check the bibliographic details.
5	I have referred to [CASP: Aims], how important is this with regard to browsing? Does the user need to know? Seems a 'red herring'.
6	I wonder if I referred to Conklin (1987) in that file. No, but I did refer to the Nagy book. No link required.

Table 2 *Author generated protocol of part of a navigation session.*

In this example the author has made two User Links at stages 2 and 3. At other stages no links were made, although the author was checking for the possible insertion of links. The browse shown above indicates that with a clear purpose in mind there are still quite a number of 'red herrings'. Such jumps are of course required by the designer. He was evaluating the relevance of the node visited. In a similar way, learners evaluate the relevance of nodes when they are accessed. In order to be able to make such assessments, the user needs some goal or focusing mechanism to provide criteria for the evaluation. Non-evaluated jumps or 'gotos' are found in Globetrotting. With implicit goals or a lack of goals browsing can produce a 'lost in hyperspace' phenomenon (see 'Lost in Hyperspace', Chapter 7). Of course, goals are not always articulated in such a clear way as above. The question the author had in mind was 'will access to this node help the user understand hypertext more fully?'. Other questions, expressed explicitly in terms of learner performance objectives for the user, might give different results.

Graphical browsing versus nodal browsing

Changes are constantly taking place in the way interfaces to hypertext systems are designed (Akscyn et al , 1988). This will present many new challenges to designers and users. Currently conventional interfaces provide sufficient challenges. It was suggested above that there is a distinction between the type of browsing occurring when the user has a graphical interface as opposed to when he is moving from node to node (e.g. card to card in HyperCard). This distinction is important here as we discuss the way we control browsing with graphical interfaces. In references to NoteCards the reader will be aware that the Grapher package can produce node-link-node graphs (see *Collaborative Writing in NoteCards*, Chapter 3). Such graphs are shown below in Figs 13 and 14. Fig 13 is an overview of the proposed book being written showing that part referred to above in the browsing example.

These browsers can be very large and contain many nodes. Different rules of thumb exist that suggest the possible number of nodes and links occurring in typical browsers. Using a NoteCard file containing 500 nodes (chunks of information as text, graphics, pictures) the user might generate a browser with 100 nodes and 200 links, each of which may be one of ten different types. Where the number of nodes exceeds the number that can reasonably be displayed in a window, it is possible to display an 'overview browser'. Such a browser is shown in Fig 14 overleaf.

This browser can be used to give a sense of the extent of a hypertext information system, without giving detail. Often the user requires to see how much more there is, or how many more nodes are available before a dead end is met. The amount of information in a graphical browser available to the user is enormous. This problem information, explosion requires some form of information reduction.

A useful way of reducing such complexity is literally to reduce the amount of information and give what McAleese (1987) and McAleese and Duncan (1987) call 'terrain knowledge'. Another technique used is the Fish-eye Browser (McAleese, 1987), Irish (1987) . This idea will be taken up below. Further, the range of possible nodes that can be visited is very large. With such a browser as an interface, each of the nodes, without some form of evaluation criteria, is equally as probable as the next node. How can the user make a choice when deciding which node to examine/visit next? One technique is to use a form of typographic cueing to distinguish one node from another; a filtering technique to minimize the amount of extraneous information being passed to the user. Filtering exists in the construction of browsers by determining the number of levels of nodes represented and the type of link and node selected.

Larson (1986) suggests a visual approach to browsing in traditional databases. Using the preprocessing operations referred to above he shows a graphical representation of data elements using a CODASYL network database. Others have attempted to produce a pictorial or graphical system to give 'terrain' views of data, eg GUIDE (Graphical User Interface for Database Exploration) see Wong and Kuo, 1982. Such attempts can be considered as complexity management techniques applied to hypertext systems. An additional technique is to use a convention to shows the link types emanating from a node in a consistent direction (eg 90° N). Such 'Compass Browsers' are still under development in Aberdeen at the time of writing. Fish-eye browsers andtypographic cueing are discussed below.

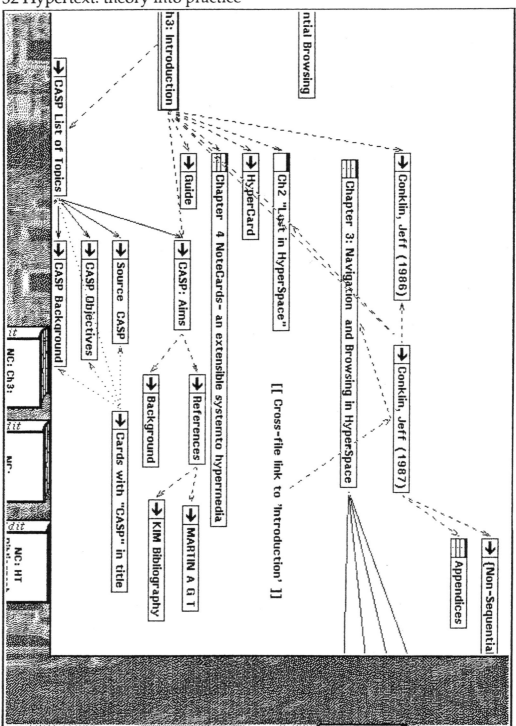

Fig 13 *Overview browser of example.*

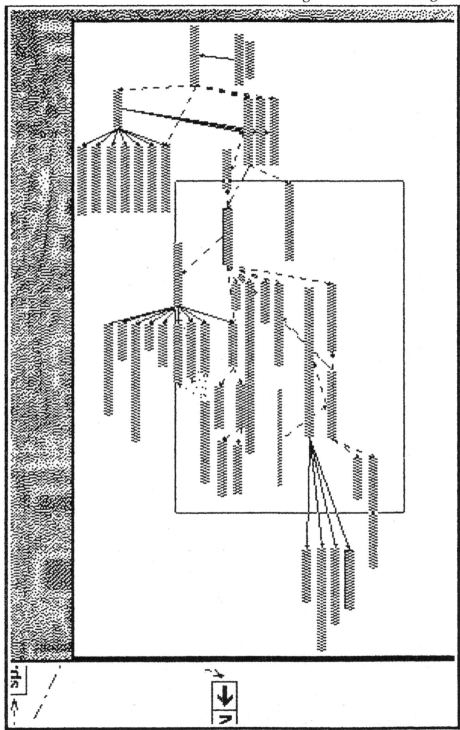

Fig 14 *Reduced terrain view of Fig 13*

Canter D, Rivers R and Storrs G.
    Address for correspondence:
    University of Surrey, Guildford, Surrey, England.
(1985) **Characterizing user navigation through complex data structures.**

Abstract

1   Introduction

2   Characterizing routes through a database

3   Experimental results

4   Interpretation
Many factors will influence user behaviour: factors related to the interface and data structure and factors the user brings with him to a particular task. Individual differences in problem-solving strategies as well as task and motivational variables are likely to influence navigational patterns. Some of the possible psychological implications of the indices have already been mentioned, for example, it might be possible to characterize 'fear of getting lost' in terms of high SQ; on the other hand, particular command systems may impose this kind of search strategy.

There are many search strategies which it might be useful to characterize using these indices in this way and Table 3 lists some possibilities. Some of the strategies suggested in the table can be discussed in more detail.

5   Applications

Acknowledgement

References

Fig 15 *Part of a Guide Document*

Fish-eye browsers

A number of research workers have devised a generalized method of displaying information using the fish-eye metaphor. In this the information display is deformed with an area of detail of 'sharp focus' and an area of reduced information or 'background' detail. Peggy Irish and Austin Henderson have developed the technique with NoteCards. The usefulness of such a system is where the number of nodes to be displayed in a graphical browser exceeds the minimum resolution of the computer screen. Although scrolling is possible, limited views from scrolled windows may promote a browser tunnel-vision. Some of the problems encountered with fish-eye views are in devising an appropriate algorithm for each task and each user. Different users tend to require different ways of reducing the amount of information.

Typographical cueing

The way the nodes in the NoteCards browser are displayed uses a bitmap icon to represent the 'node'. A bitmap can be altered to give different forms. Many different types of icon can be used in a browser to indicate different functions of hypertext elements. The File Box icon can be used to suggest a collection of further items. Other icons are not as descriptive in this instance, but can be associated with different levels of detail or items containing bibliographic information, media or guidelines. The lines used to indicate the path from node to node are also differentiated. Lines of different strength and pattern can be used to indicate main paths, minor paths, etc.

Typographical cueing can be applied to text interfaces as well as graphical interfaces. Guide™ versions of lengthy articles or 'books' use such cueing (see Chapter 6, *Design Issues in Large Hypertext Systems for Technical Documentation*). The example in Fig 14 shows some of the cueing used in Guide. Here a journal article (Canter *et al*, 1985) has been turned into a hypertext document. Simple but effective cueing is used. The 'folded' elements are displayed in bold characters, eg 'Table 3'. Further, when the cursor moves over such 'hot spots' it changes shape from the standard vertical bar to a crosshair. Graphical browsers, text frames and even cursors can be used to indicate the nature of the task and thus facilitate browsing.

Summary

This chapter aimed to give a Cooks Tour of the concepts related to browsing and navigation. With this in mind here is a summary of the points made in the chapter.

- Browsing is an active information seeking activity.

- Browsing should be purposeful.

- Structure imposed on what is browsed or on the process of browsing facilitates effective browsing. Users must have some knowledge of structure to build on.

- Hierarchical structures can be created from network structures by deforming (elongating) the net structure. This deformation can provide a useful scaffolding to give the user some orientation during browsing.

- Browsing is a member of a set of information seeking activities or strategies best suited to covering a large and complex area without going into too much detail.

- Browsing can be enhanced using a variety of tools to help the user keep track of events.

- Browsing can facilitate discovery learning by providing the ideational scaffolding while allowing learners to find out for themselves.

- Hypertext facilitates an explosive increase in information. Such complexity can be managed when clear goals for activities are explicit.

- Browsing requires personal and system filtering mechanisms to tailor the information presented to the needs of the user.

- Overviews can be deformed using a fish-eye view to provide both 'terrain' and 'street' views.

- Typographic and iconic cues can be used to direct the attention of the user and to draw distinctions between node and links of different types, eg {Summary nodes}, [see for an example] links.

References

Akscyn R *et al* (1988) The data model is the heart of interface design. Proceedings of ACM CHI '88, Washington, DC, 15-19 May.

Ausubel D (1974) *School learning: an introduction to educational psychology.* Holt Rinehart and Winston, London.

Batley S (1989) Visual information retrieval: browsing strategies in pictorial databases. Unpublished PhD thesis, University of Aberdeen.

Belkin N J and Vickery A (1985) Interaction in information systems: a review of research from document retrieval to knowledge-based systems. *Library and Information Research Report 35*. British Library.

Bourne L E and Restle F (1959) Mathematical theory of concept identification, *Psychological Review* 66, pp 278-296.

Bush V (1945) As we may think. *Atlantic Monthly* 176, pp 101-108.

Canter D, Rivers R and Storrs G (1985) Characterizing user navigation through complex data structures. *Behaviour and Information Technology* 4 (2): 93-102.

Conklin J (1987) Hypertext: an introduction and survey. *IEEE Computer* 20 (9): 17-41.

Fisher K *et al* (1987) SemNet. University of Davis, California, Mimeo.

Foss C L (1987) Effective browsing in hypertext systems. Unpublished Paper, University of Lancaster.

Halasz F G, Moran T P and Trigg R H (1987) NoteCards in a nutshell. *Proceedings of the ACM CHI+GI Conference*, Toronto. pp 45-52.

Hammond N V and Allinson L J (1988) Travels around a learning support environment: rambling, orienteering or touring? In: CHI '88 Conference Proceedings: *Human Factors in Computer Systems*. Washington, May. Edited by Soloway E, Frye D and Sheppard S B. ACM Press, New York. pp 269-273.

Hildreth C (1982) The concept and mechanics of browsing in an online library catalogue. In: *Proceedings of the 3rd National Online Meeting*. Learned Information.

Ingwersen P (1986) Cognitive analysis and the role of the intermediary in information retrieval. In: *Intelligent Information Systems: Progress and Prospects*. Edited by Davies R. Ellis Horwood.

Irish P (1987) *Fish-eye browsers*. Xerox Palo Alto Research Center, Coyote Hill, Palo Alto, California, Mimeo.

Larson J A (1986) A visual approach to browsing in a database environment. *Computer (IEEE)*. pp 62-71.

McAleese R (1986) Cognitive factors influencing authors in a CBL system. *Proceedings of 5th Canadian Symposium on Instructional Technology*, 5-7 May, Ottawa. pp 113-117.

McAleese R (1987) The graphical representation of knowledge as an interface to knowledge based systems. In: *Human Computer Interaction*. Edited by Bullinger H J and Shackel B. North Holland. pp 1089-1093.

McAleese R and Duncan E B (1987) The graphical representation of 'terrain' and 'street' knowledge in an interface to a database system. *Proceedings of 11th International Online Meeting*, Learned Information. pp 443-546.

Monk A F et al (1988) A comparison of hypertext, scrolling and folding as mechanisms for program browsing. Paper presented at *Hypertext 1*, University Teaching Centre, Aberdeen, 1988.

Morse P M (1973) Browsing and search theory. In: *Toward a Theory of Librarianship*: papers in honour of Jesse Hauk Shera. Edited by Rawski C. Scarecrow Press.

Mylonos K (1988) *Personal communication*, MIT, Boston.

Nelson T H (1981) *Literary Machines*. San Antonio, Texas.

Nelson T H (1988) Managing immense storage. *Byte*, 225-238.

Oddy R N (1977) Information retrieval through man-machine dialogue. *Journal of Documentation* 33 (1): 1-14.

O'Connor B C (1985) Access to moving image documents: background concepts and proposals for surrogates for film and video works. *Journal of Documentation* 41 (4): 209-220.

Palay A J and Fox M S (1981) Browsing through databases. In: *Information Retrieval Research*. Edited by Oddy R N et al. Butterworth.

Pask G and Scott B C E (1972) Learning strategies and individual competence. *International Journal of Man-Machine Studies* 4. pp 217-253.

Pask G (1974) *Conversation Theory*. Academic Press, London.

Rhode N F (1986) Information needs. In: *Advances in Librarianship*. Vol 14. Edited by Simonton W. Academic Press.

Rummelhart D E and Norman D A (1981) Analogical processes in learning. In: *Cognitive skills and their acquisition*. Edited by Anderson J R. Lawrence Erlbaum, New Jersey.

Salton G (Editor) (1971) *The SMART Retrieval System - Experiments in Automatic Document Processing*. Prentice-Hall.

Trigg R and Weiser M (1986) TEXTNET: a network based approach to text handling. *ACM Transactions on Office Information Systems* 4 (1).

Weyer S A (1982) The design of a dynamic book for information search. *International Journal of Man-Machine Studies*. 17 (1): 87-10

Wong H K and Kuo I (1982) GUIDE: graphical user interface for database exploration. *Proceedings of the Eighth VLDB*, Mexico City.

Notes

[1]   A version of this chapter was given in a presentation at an ASLIB conference on Hypertext, 30th June 1988, London.

[2]   An extensive survey of browsing relevant to hypertext is to be found in Batley, S (1989) Visual Information Retrieval: Browsing Strategies in Pictorial Databases, unpublished PhD, University of Aberdeen. The author is grateful to Sue Batley for the work she did in reviewing the research in this field.

[3]   The distinction being made here is between the HyperCard systems, Type 1 (Chapter 5) and the NoteCard systems, Type 2 (Chapter 3).

[4]   The system consists of a LAN with Xerox AI workstations running NoteCards; an Amiga 2000 with interactive video and an Apple Mac II.

[5]   A number of phases of design have been identified in on-going research. This research is part of the Alvey interactive initiative in the UK. The project (MMI 110) is concerned with the construction of intelligent interfaces to information systems using interactive video. Part of the research concerns the capture of domain knowledge in the authoring process. This research is attempting to classify some of the link types that exist in domain knowledge. Different stages of modes of link creation have been identified. Different link types exist. The examples in this chapter are drawn from some early work (in 1988). In this the link types can be classified into a number of general categories: Semantic, Pedagogic and Designer. Designer links are in existence in the notefile. The author is putting in User Links. In NoteCards, diferent modes are possible. Each mode can have associated with it, different sets of links, e.g. Designer, Learner.

3

Randall H Trigg
Lucy A Suchman[1]

Collaborative writing in NoteCards

Abstract

A description of the NoteCards hypertext system and its development with
collaborative notefiles. The chapter explains the nature of hypertext collaboration
with the development of message cards. Implications for hypertext designers are
drawn.

Background

In recent years there has been increasing recognition among system designers that
human activity is basically interactive in nature. Among other things, this has led
to widespread attempts to provide computer support for collaborative work
(CSCW, 1986 and Greif, 1988). At the same time, interest in hypertext or
hypermedia systems has blossomed following the success of a few large-scale
research hypertext systems as well as several commercially available products.
(For overviews of work in this area, see Conklin, 1987 and Hypertext, 1987).
Among other application areas, hypertext has recently been used to support
writers (Trigg and Irish, 1987 and Smith and Lansman, 1988). What we have not
seen to date is a concerted study of computer-supported collaborative writing, and
of the value of hypertext as supporting technology. The work presented here by no
means represents such a study, however, we have taken one small step in that
direction by attempting to use the NoteCards hypertext system to support our
own collaborative work. In what follows, we describe the NoteCards system, our
experience using it in the writing process, and several design implications.

NoteCards

NoteCards is a hypertext system developed at Xerox PARC some five years ago
(Halasz *et al*, 1987). Like other hypertext or hypermedia systems, NoteCards can be
thought of as a network-based information-structuring tool. NoteCards has been
used for a wide variety of applications ranging from instructional design to project
management, from legal argumentation to engineering design. One of its major

strengths is its tailorability, the capacity for users to extend the system in ways appropriate for their application and personal style (Trigg *et al*, 1987). The nodes in a NoteCards network are called 'cards' and contain pieces of text, graphics, video, animation, etc. These are connected by typed links which capture relationships between nodes. So, for example, if the text in one card provides support for an argument appearing in another card, the two cards would be connected by a support link. Fig 1 shows two text cards, as well as a filebox and a browser card. (For the moment, the reader need not be concerned with the content/context of these cards.) The text card titled 'voice and agency' contains a link to the card titled 'Thoughts with L on 1:00:05-1:20:10'. Fileboxes, such as the one titled 'observations', provide a means for embedding hierarchical structures in a NoteCards network. Cards can be filed in multiple fileboxes and fileboxes can themselves be filed in other fileboxes. At the top of Fig 1 is a Browser card which provides an active 'diagram' of some portion of the network. Links of different types are shown using a variety of dash styles.

A collaborative notefile

Over the last two years, NoteCards has been used to support collaborators working in asynchronous or draft-passing settings (Trigg *et al*, 1986). In one case, the authors (a Computer Scientist and an Anthropologist) have been using NoteCards as the medium for a shared project notebook in which we keep notes from readings, videotape transcriptions and analysis, as well as papers and talks. But another way to think of what is called our 'notefile' is as the record of an ongoing dialogue. At the time of writing this paper, we are in the midst of drafting a paper documenting a study of two AI researchers working at a whiteboard. Fig 2 shows three stages of our progress captured in three fileboxes. We used the box on the left for gathering materials relevant to the project, including videotape analyses, notes, discussions, etc. Next, we constructed an organization of the materials corresponding to an issue-based outline of the paper. More recently, we built a third organization for a transcript-based outline. (Note that all three organizations coexist in the notefile, while at the same time sharing large numbers of cards.) In what follows, we briefly discuss each of these structures in turn.

Fig 3 shows some of the materials used for the paper. In the upper right is a card reminding us of various questions we need to ask one of the scientists we are studying.

Below that is a card containing the results of the interview eventually conducted. The Fishmarket is a popular restaurant near Xerox PARC where we had a dinner meeting. Lucy later transferred our meeting notes from a paper placemat into the notefile. A somewhat different 'boundary crossing' is visible in the cards on the left of Fig 3. Using a special card type called File card, we were able to create links to external files created by the scientists we are studying (who are not themselves NoteCards users). Following a link to such a card brings up the contents of the file in a notecard window just as if the file's contents were part of the notefile.

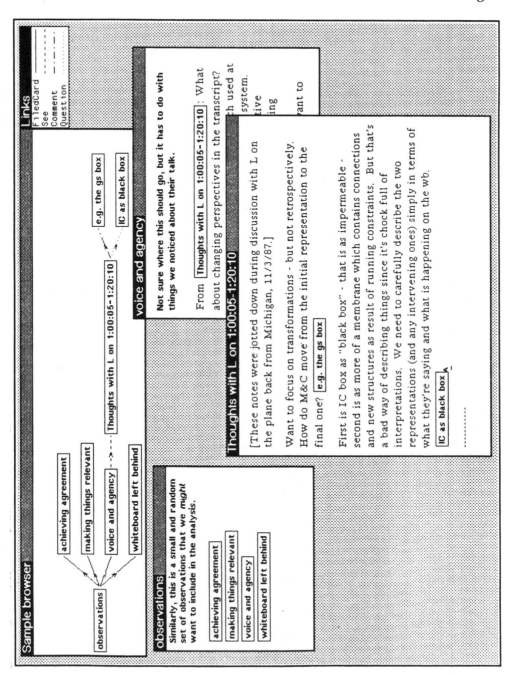

Fig 1 *Several cards and a browser*

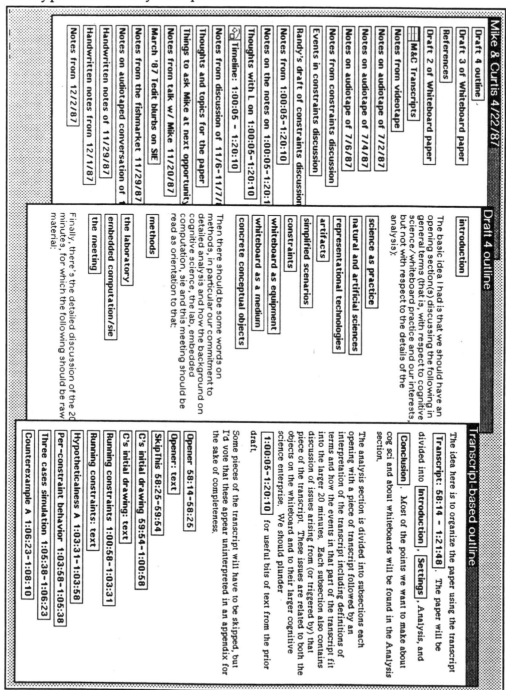

Fig 2 *Three overlapping structures*

Fig 4 shows some of the cards making up the issue-based outline. Note the description of each issue followed by links to relevant cards and initial text. In addition, some text has been copied directly from a prior draft of the paper. In the transcript-based outline shown in Fig 5, each top-level card contains a bit of transcript from our videotape followed by notes on what we should say in that section of the paper. For a few of these, text has been composed.[2]

But in what sense is the notefile supporting collaboration? What forms of interaction take place in such an online environment? Most simply, the notefile provides a shared workspace so that when working independently, we each have access to the product of the others' work. We explicitly use each others' work, for example, by referring in our own cards to the other's cards via the linking facilities (eg in Fig 4, Randy's card 'Artificial social order?' comments on Lucy's 'natural and artificial sciences'), or by copying the contents from the other's card into our own. Furthermore, we can respond to each others' work in a more complex and extended way than is practical with previous writing technologies. In addition to the usual commentary that takes place with any form of draft-passing, annotations in NoteCards can lead to dialogues within the medium itself. In Fig 6, the three cards titled 'Thoughts and topics for the paper', 'relation to other fields', and 'Whiteboards in cog sci and other fields', comprise such a dialogue.

History cards

Our draft-passing style of collaborative writing quickly led to the problem of how to locate changes made since one's last session in the notefile. As a solution, we devised a facility called History cards (Trigg *et al*, 1986). A History card records the work in a single session pointing one's collaborator at the scene of most recent activity, including the latest turns in ongoing discussions. Fig 6 shows two history cards linked to portions of an ongoing dialogue. The upper history card titled '11/25/87 L' records Lucy's work during a session in late November, 1987. Among other activities, she read and annotated the card 'Thoughts and topics for the paper' with links to various comments. During Randy's next session in December, he continued the dialogue by responding to her query in 'relation to other fields' with a link to a new card 'Whiteboards in cog sci and other fields'. A second link to the new card can be found in that session's history card titled '12/6/87 R'. By first bringing up this history card in her next session, Lucy gains instant access to the most recent changes to the notefile. Moreover, the ever-expanding list of history cards (filed chronologically in the filebox on the left in Fig 6) provides a temporal organization of the contents of the notefile in addition to whatever other organizations are already present (eg the outline-based organizations of Fig 2).

Message cards and the convention adoption process

Sharing the notefile requires that we come to agreement on certain of our work practices - on not only what's in the notefile, but on how we are going to use it. We've found, moreover, that there is a structure to those discussions which begin with a question or proposal and end with the adoption (and occasionally

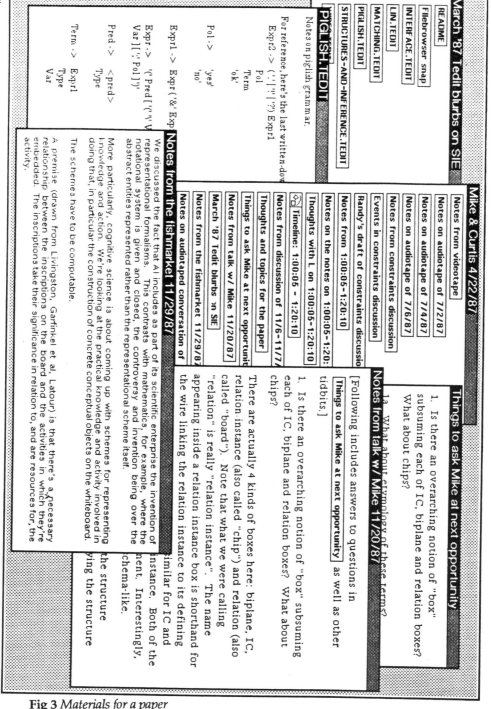

Fig 3 *Materials for a paper*

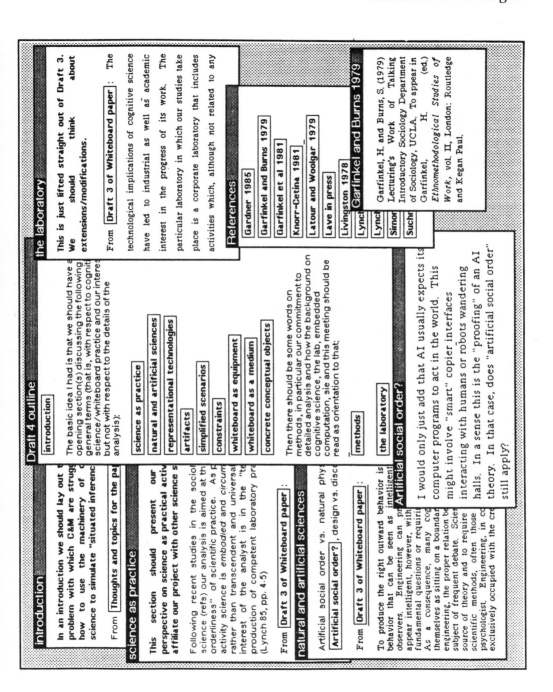

Fig 4 *Issue-based organisation*

automation) of a convention for using the medium. Our needs as users were adopted after discussion within the medium. As the convention became both agreeable and routine, we partially automated it by tailoring NoteCards. The first step was to automate the creation, titling and filing of a history card upon opening the notefile. More recently, the filling-in of history cards has been semi-automated (Irish and Trigg, 1989).

We invented Message cards in order to support the kind of discussion characterizing the convention adoption process. Such 'meta-discussion' differs from annotation in that it is not generally attached to a particular card. Fig 7 shows several message cards each titled with the date, initial of the author, and a brief indication of content. Like the subject lines of electronic mail messages, titles of message cards in an ongoing dialogue each refer to the topic of discussion. Here we see part of a discussion on the use of fonts which in turns leads to proposals for conventions on card titling.

When to start a meta-discussion

An important aspect of these interactions involves the question of what counts as a candidate for discussion. Certain actions taken without remark in one's own notefile can become issues that need to be discussed in a collaborative setting. For example, the message card appearing in Fig 8 communicates Lucy's decision that a card (titled 'Forms of interaction') she created earlier is now ripe for removal. In her own personal notefile, she would delete such a card directly. In this collaborative context, however, she feels the need to check with her collaborator on the chance that he may have a different approach to dealing with outdated cards. Though she created the card, it has now become common property, part of the shared notefile, and thus its removal becomes a subject for negotiation. In this case, the negotiation results in agreement on a new filebox, in which we can store outdated cards.

The adoption of a given practice requires discussion insofar as one can't assume that the practice is already shared. That is, while Lucy might see deletions as something requiring explicit agreement, she has no hesitation about, for example, structuring her text cards into paragraphs. Our collaborative work involves that, and many other practices that we have never discussed explicitly. In this respect, our collaboration makes use of two kinds of conventions: those that we inherit from the larger community (eg conventions for structuring text); and those that we create in response to the requirements of interaction in this particular environment. The former we simply do, without any explicit mention. For the latter, we need a mechanism for negotiation.

Implications for hypertext designers

While conscious of the dangers of extrapolating from our own experience, we can see experience of other writers in NoteCards. First, we believe that there may be general features of hypertext that make it appropriate for collaborative writing. For example, hypertext systems support the coexistence of multiple overlapping

Transcript-based outline

The idea here is to organize the paper using the tr...

[Transcript: 58:14 - 1:21:48]. The paper will

[Introduction], [Settings], Analysis, and [Concl...
points we want to make about cog sci and about wh...
found in the Analysis section.

The analysis section is divided into subsections ea...
piece of transcript followed by an interpretation o...
including definitions of terms and how the events
transcript fit into the larger 20 minutes. Each sub...
discussion of issues arising from (or triggered by) I
transcript. These issues are related to both the obj...
whiteboard and to their larger cognitive science en...
plunder [1:00:05-1:20:10] for useful bits of tex...

Some pieces of the transcript will have to
these appear uninterpreted in an appendi...

[Opener 58:14-58:25]

[Opener: text]

[SkipThis 58:25-59:54]

[C's initial drawing 59:54-1:00:58]

[C's initial drawing: text]

[Running constraints 1:00:58-1:03:31]

[Running constraints: text]

[Hypotheticalness A 1:03:31-1:03:58]

[Per-constraint behavior 1:03:58-1:0...]

[Three cases simulation 1:05:38-1:06]

[Counterexample A 1:06:23-1:08:10]

[Hypotheticalness B 1:08:10-1:08:20]

[Counterexample B 1:08:20-1:10:06]

[Nature of constraints 1:10:06-1:11:...]

C's initial drawing 59:54-1:00:58

different than the ones appearing on computers: relative advantages and disadvantages, e.g. communicative efficacy vs computability, etc,

Issues - cog sci:_

Might start with bits from [concrete conceptual objects] and [whiteboard objects]

See also [box terminology note].

Tell story about relation of wb to computer, translatable to computer and "testable" the code that runs scheduling..." Take bits from [whiteboard as a medium].

Tell story (if any) about constraints using b...

C's initial drawing: text

[piece of transcript 59:54 - 1:00:58]

[Make this paragraph into a footnote?] The above transcript actually occurs some thirty seconds after the end of the preceding segment. In the interests of space, we have omitted an analysis of ...nt. (See Appendix xx for the missing

...ter of some significance that in the
...e minute, C is able to represent on the
...(with M's agreement) the objects
...the remainder of the twenty minute
...under our scrutiny. As this indicates,
...tart from a basic agreement about the
...locks of their representations and
...mediately move on to the subject matter
...rns them, namely the behavior of these
...hose concerns will lead them to
...ore closely the relationship between

Hypotheticalness A 1:03:31-1:03:58

M: But my sense is that what we want to do is, imagine that there is a meeting.

(1.0)

C: Oh yea:h, //that's, that exactly//

M: //And then uh// see what the consequences of that are, I mean that seems like the //right way to frame (inaudible)//

C: //Right and the consequences// are that Tore is a graduate student in this case,

M: Well. if we, /if we treat that//

C: //So we have to verify that that's the reality.

Interpretation:

Explain how they view the isolated context box as a hypothetical. Also explain how this is the first of several returns to the hypotheticalness assumption over the course of the meeting.

Issues - whiteboard:

Fig 5 *A transcript-based outline*

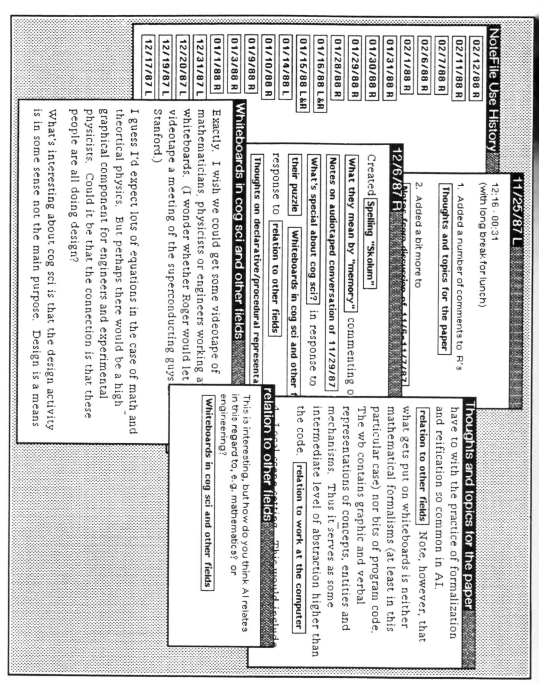

Fig 6 *History cards*

Comment

I think that we should just adopt the convention of always having our comments be linked cards, inserted at the appropriate point. That's easy enough to do, and gets us the date info for free.

`<Response> Agreed`

Agreed

I agree. Let's go for links to all comments. Perhaps when we create guided tours of the notefile for first time readers, we could "flatten" some of these commentary structures into single cards.

(Also, see my message
`2/16/86 R: On titles for comment cards` .)

2/16/86 R: On titles for comment cards

I'd like to propose a convention for our comments and responses to each other's cards and comment cards. Currently, we tend to title the card "Comment" or "Response" or "Question" and use a link type of the same name. Seems redundant. How about if we make "Comment," etc, the link type and give it some more communicative title?

Agreed

Yes. Let's do as you propose. I've added a card recording the decision
`Titles for comment cards` , to the filebox
`Decisions on notefile use` .

Messages

`README`

`1/28/86 L: fonts`

`1/28/86 L: Conventions`

`1/30/86 R: Re: fonts`

1/28/86 L: fonts

Does it make sense for each of us to use a different font for our entries? I find myself wanting to do so for two reasons. First, I personally prefer Helvetica 10 to Timesroman 12. More importantly, it makes immediately evident who wrote what. We could argue about whether the latter is desirable or not—my inclination is to say that it is, in that it makes this Notefile an ongoing dialogue between us, rather than a joint production in the sense that we would want if we wrote a paper together. At this stage I think our collaboration is a dialogue; that is, the object of it and the benefit that we get is in being able to respond to each other's ideas, rather than having to produce a single document. Thoughts?

1/30/86 R: Re: fonts

I think the fonts idea is great. I like knowing instantly which of us wrote what I'm looking at.

Here's my worry, though. How can we tell in what time order each of our commentary occurred within a card? It would be easy if we knew that new commentary always was appended to the bottom of the card. That might not be appropriate, however if, say, your last comment makes a point that I want to respond to in its vicinity.

Might a reasonable convention be as follows? Try to add our next comment at the bottom of a card if possible. If not, consider creating a link to it from the appropriate point. (Easy to get dates off of that card.) Only if that's not appropriate (comment is too short to make linking worth the effort) do we insert new text inside existing text.

`Comment`

Fig 7 *Message cards*

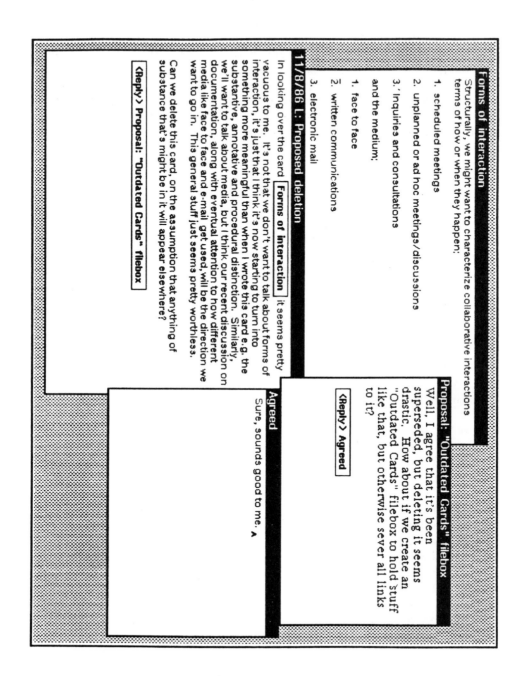

Forms of interaction

Structurally, we might want to characterize collaborative interactions in terms of how or when they happen:

1. scheduled meetings

2. unplanned or ad hoc meetings/discussions

3.' Inquiries and consultations

and the medium;

1. face to face

2. written communications

3. electronic mail

11/8/86 L: Proposed deletion

In looking over the card | Forms of interaction | it seems pretty vacuous to me. It's not that we don't want to talk about forms of interaction, it's just that I think it's now starting to turn into something more meaningful than when I wrote this card e.g. the substantive, annotative and procedural distinction. Similarly, we'll want to talk about media, but I think our recent discussion on documentation, along with eventual attention to how different media like face to face and e-mail get used, will be the direction we want to go in. This general stuff just seems pretty worthless.

| <Reply> Proposal: "Outdated Cards" filebox |

Can we delete this card, on the assumption that anything of substance that's might be in it will appear elsewhere?

Proposal: "Outdated Cards" filebox

Well, I agree that it's been superseded, but deleting it seems drastic. How about if we create an "Outdated Cards" filebox to hold stuff like that, but otherwise sever all links to it?

| <Reply> Agreed |

Agreed

Sure, sounds good to me. ▲

Fig 8 *Negotiating the deletion of a card*

organizations of information. This is in contrast to outline processors in which only one organization at a time can be entertained. Such multiple organizations may be especially useful if authors are in the process of progressively reorganising their work (as in Fig 2), or if they elect to maintain two or more outlines of a developing paper in parallel. Hypertext is also well suited for the annotating activities typical of paper draft-passing. (Note that there are systems that support online draft-passing without hypertext. See for example Leland *et al*, 1988.)

Annotation, however, is just one way that collaborators working through a draft-passing process need to refer to each other's work. A full understanding of the possibilities for remote reference is still to come, but the evidence from early prototypes is intriguing. For example, history cards seem to provide a useful means for grouping references to temporally clustered work. Guided tours and what are called 'table tops' provide another way of directing the reader's attention in the context of creating self-documenting notefiles.

Perhaps the main lesson to be learned from our experience is the importance of supporting users' adaptation of the technology. In the collaborative case, this may require discussion among collaborators at a level removed from the subject matter of their work. While the relative time spent on procedural versus substantive work may be small, the acceptability of the technology could depend crucially on the ease with which users can adapt it to their own work ways discovered in the course of working together.

References

Conklin J (1987) Hypertext: an introduction and survey. *IEEE Computer* 20 (9): 17-41.

CSCW '86 (1986) *Proceedings of the Conference on Computer-Supported Cooperative Work.* December 3-5, Austin, Texas.

Halasz F G, Moran T P and Trigg R H (1987) Notecards in a nutshell. *Proceedings of the ACM CHI+GI Conference*, Toronto. pp 45-52.

Hypertext '87 Planning Committee (1987) *Hypertext '87 Papers.* November 13-15. Chapel Hill, North Carolina.

Irene Greif (Editor) (1988) *Computer-Supported Cooperative Work: a book of readings.* Morgan - Kaufman.

Irish P M and Trigg R H (1989) Supporting collaboration in hypermedia: issues and experiences. *Journal of the American Society of Information Science.*

Leland M D P, Fish R S and Kraut R E (1988) Collaborative document production using quilt. *Proceedings of the Conference on Computer-Supported Cooperative Work*, September 26-28, Portland, Oregon.

Smith J B and Lansman M (1988) *A cognitive basis for a computer writing environment.* University of North Carolina at Chapel Hill, TR87-032, June, 1988.

Trigg R H, Suchman L and Halasz F G (1986) Supporting collaboration in NoteCards. *Proceedings of the Conference on Computer-Supported Cooperative Work*,

December 3-5. Austin, Texas.

Trigg R H and Irish P M (1987) Hypertext habitats: experiences of writers in NoteCards. *Hypertext '87 Papers*, November 13-15. Chapel Hill, North Carolina.

Trigg R H, Moran T P and Halasz F G (1987) Adaptability and tailorability in NoteCards. In: *Human-Computer Interaction - INTERACT '87*. Edited by Bullinger H J and Shackel B. Elsevier Science Publishers BV, North-Holland.

Notes

[1]   Many thanks to Peggy Irish and Randy Gobbel, our colleagues on the collaborative NoteCards project.

[2]   The writing style used in our notefile is but one of a wide variety of styles in evidence in the NoteCards user community. Trigg and Irish (1987) document a study of researchers using NoteCards for writing. In that study, writing is viewed broadly as including notetaking, structuring and restructuring materials, and creating references and bibliographies, as well as final text composition and draft preparation.

Lesley Allinson
Nick Hammond

A learning support environment: the hitch-hiker's guide

Abstract

The philosophy, realisation and evaluation of a learning support environment for non-formal knowledge domains is described. Emphasis is placed on the need to provide a variety of access structures and on the use of a travel holiday metaphor as a means of helping users understand the system model.

Introduction[1]

Learning Support Environments (LSEs) provide the learner with a set of tools to support the exploration of knowledge domains. An LSE should permit the user to employ their most effective strategies for learning within an appropriate context - and it should be remembered that 'context' includes not only the material and structure of the knowledge domain in question, but also the user's current learning needs.

In this paper, we outline the development and underlying psychological principles of an LSE for non-formal domains. Though originally developed as a supporting aid in the teaching of Cognitive Psychology at a university level, the approach has been extended into other areas - for example, a package about the history of York. The supporting authoring tools mean that the system can be employed for a wide range of domains.

Many candidate user groups, including our undergraduate Psychology students, are not generally proficient at using computers. Indeed, our own students are often further alienated through their interaction with various statistical packages which bear all the hallmarks of a traditional mainframe interface. So we realized that if the voluntary use of an LSE was to be successful, then the system must be useful in extending the student's knowledge and understanding, and it must be easy to use so as not to squander the student's resources on learning the system *per se*.

Hypertext-based presentation interfaces have been advocated as a basis for such learning applications (Conklin,1987), but there is some evidence, often of an anecdotal nature, of problems with hypertext systems. Users may get lost, or at least experience difficulty finding specific information. Also, a particular problem is that users may ramble through the knowledge base in an unmotivated and inefficient fashion, unable to forge the linkages between the individual information screens and hence discover the underlying concepts which hold together and structure isolated knowledge 'fragments'. Our solution to these possible problems is to provide a wide range of access structures. Furthermore, as an aid for the novice user to understand the purpose and function of these access aids and hence provide an overall understanding of the system model, extensive use has been made of a travel holiday metaphor.

Non-formal knowledge domains

Many knowledge domains are not formal in a strict sense such as most of those within mathematics or the physical sciences, but there is often an underlying structure which holds together the 'raw data' of the domain. The strength and nature of this structure, or set of linkages, often varies within a particular domain. Psychology, as with many areas of knowledge, contains controversy, conflicting explanations of the same experimental evidence, historical perspectives, personal opinions, as well as 'hard facts'. All these factors make the precise modelling of the knowledge domain impossible. There is no single route to a unique answer, but what is inherent in a deep understanding of these non-formal domains is the ability to organize and structure the material by isolating the main points and forming the necessary connections between related items.

A programmed learning environment would not be appropriate for this type of domain, as it would prevent the student from developing their own critical abilities in coping with (often) conflicting information and explanations. An LSE which concentrates on the main points of the knowledge domain, and makes the connections or allows the students to form them, would be the more applicable. In this we are fortunate in that the strengths of the microcomputer match our educational requirements. Microcomputers are good in providing flexible and powerful mechanisms for accessing material, but they are a poor medium for presenting large amounts of text. We have discussed previously the other strengths of microcomputer presentation which can be exploited (Hammond and Allinson, 1988).

Educational context

This particular LSE was not intended to replace conventional lectures or extensive reading of the literature, but was to be integrated into the traditional educational environment. Users are liable, therefore, to have some basic minimum knowledge about the topic in question before they use the system. However, the users' existing knowledge base will vary considerably, as will their requirements of the system (eg initial exploration of a topic, preparing for an essay, examination revision) and their individual learning strategies. Hence the system must be flexible in control both over the sequencing of the learning materials and over the types of learning activity. Traditional approaches to computer-assisted learning present little in the way of control over the sequencing of the materials and nothing in the control over learning activities. An archetypal hypertext system can provide great flexibility over the sequencing of the material, but without the provision of overlying navigation tools it can do little to assist the varying learning strategies of individual users. It is this matching between the learner's needs, abilities and strategies and the optimal level of control which we have attempted to address in the design of the Hitch-Hiker's Guide.

Psychological principles

The psychological literature concerning learning is vast, but little of the work has been considered within a computer-based environment. Here we can but mention some of the main underlying principles which we have employed in our design philosophy. For further discussion see Hammond and Allinson (1988).

- Encoding specificity - material can be recalled if it contains distinctive retrieval cues that can be generated at the time of recall.

- Encoding variability - multiple exposure to the same material in different contexts will result in easier recall since the varied contexts will result in a greater number of potential retrieval cues.

- Knowledge assimilation and integration - we build up our knowledge base by attaching new information to a existing knowledge structure and make constant minor alterations to this structure in order to accommodate this new information. Understanding and learning will be enhanced if students can relate new material to that which they already possess. Students should be encouraged to form these relationships and to develop frameworks for their knowledge.

- Depth of processing - in general, the more a student thinks about and explores the meaning of the material presented, the greater will be their understanding.

- Learner control - there is a complex relationship between the learner, the learning materials and the learner's goals. Learners need control over this, choosing their own behaviour patterns to ensure maximum facilitation of learning.

Different students or the same students with advancing familiarity with the material or with differing needs will adopt different learning strategies. This has been suggested by the serialist-holist dichotomy of Pask and Scott (1972). Students can also be classified as deep, shallow or strategic processors (Entwistle, 1987). The students' approach may well be changed by the importance they place or interest they have in the current task. The design of an LSE should therefore cater for these differences in students and their goals.

To capitalize on these underlying principles would require the following system features:

- Distinctive and multiple forms of representation provided by the use of graphical and dynamic presentation;

- Rich access structure with many cross links for integration;
- Ability to juxtapose materials to help integration;

- Dynamic models, interactive demonstrations and multiple-choice questions to stimulate active learning;

- Learner control over what to learn and how to learn it so as to best suit their particular goals.

System realization

Armed with our educational aims and psychological principles, we were in a position to specify our prototype LSE. The authoring component of the system permits the teacher to define a large network of display frames. The author also specifies which of a number of mechanisms are made available to students for accessing the frames. As we wished to promote active rather than passive learning, a number of multiple-choice quizzes, interactive demonstrations and selected experiments are also included. The system is capable of interpreting user activity and hence provide conditional branching to different frames, and display the results of the experimental or quiz performance in the form of either numerical data or graphical representation.

The user interface is entirely mouse-driven, and each display frame consists of a main display area with a variable number of mouse-selectable areas. These define 'hypertext links' to related frames, traversed by 'clicking' over the selectable area. In addition, there is a single line at the bottom of the screen consisting of mouse-selectable generic facilities for access and guidance, namely, help, index, map, back-one, restart, further reading, quiz, end session. The actions of each of these are fairly self-evident, however further details are given in Hammond and Allinson (1988). A typical information screen from the 'History of York' module is shown in Fig 1. The mouse selectable items include not only the bottom line boxes but also the hypertext links in the text - here underlined for clarity but in practice highlighted in yellow text.

The system is implemented on a network of Research Machines Nimbus microcomputers. These are MS-DOS machines with the capability of producing fast colour graphics with a resolution of 640 x 250 and four colours (plus textures) from a palette of 16. The network stations are connected via a 0.8 Mbaud serial local area network to a hard-disk based file server. At present there are 10 disk-less nodes plus a couple of more powerful nodes for software and courseware development.

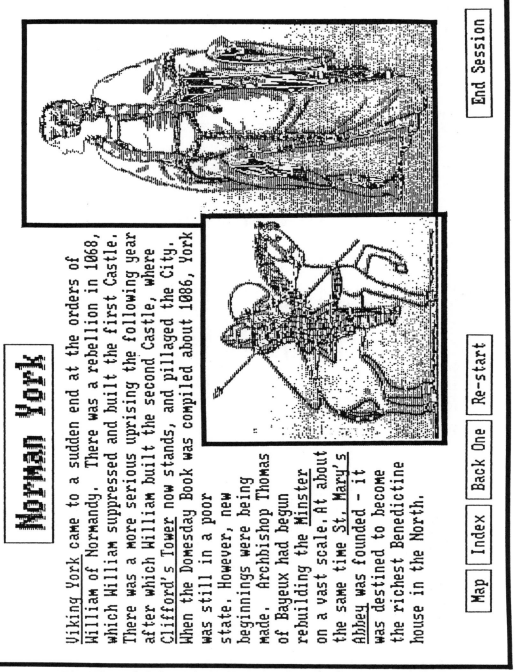

Norman York

End Session

Viking York came to a sudden end at the orders of William of Normandy. There was a rebellion in 1068, which William suppressed and built the first Castle. There was a more serious uprising the following year after which William built the second Castle, where Clifford's Tower now stands, and pillaged the City. When the Domesday Book was compiled about 1086, York was still in a poor state. However, new beginnings were being made. Archbishop Thomas of Bayeux had begun rebuilding the Minster on a vast scale. At about the same time St. Mary's Abbey was founded – it was destined to become the richest Benedictine house in the North.

Map   Index   Back One   Re-start

Fig 1 *Example information screen, taken from the History of York module, illustrating hypertext links (underlined here: colour-coded in the system) and the bottom-line boxes.*

58

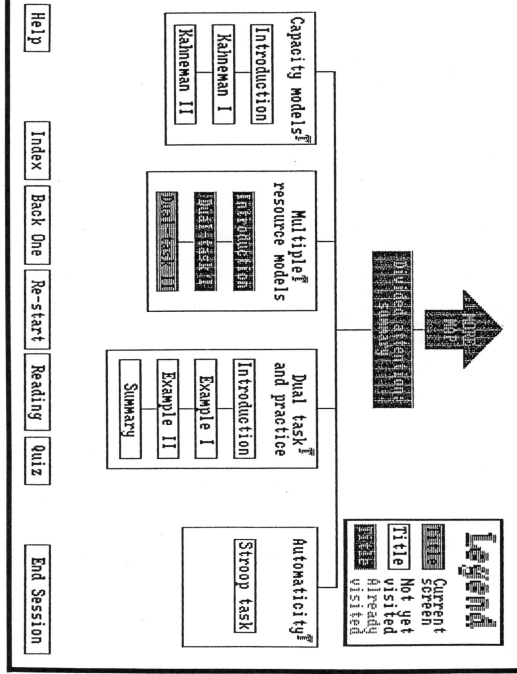

Fig 2 *Example map screen, taken from the Cognitive Psychology module, illustrating network structure and indicating which screens have been visited, and the screen from where the map was evoked. Selection of any rectangle results in the display of the associated frame.*

The travel holiday metaphor

Though free user-initiated selection through the network of display frames is always possible, there are occasions when a particular sequencing of information is desirable if not essential. The flow of an argument, steps in the discovery of a theory, chronological development of ideas or steps in an experiment all require sequential unravelling. Also, the novice user will require more structured guidance through the network than the experienced user. Hence we have introduced the notion of a guided tour. In order to aid the initial learning and use of the system, the metaphor of a travel holiday is employed. The theoretical basis of metaphor use is discussed in detail in Hammond and Allinson (1987), but generally we believe the use of a metaphor aids the user to form their internal model of the system more easily.

The main tutorial mechanism is the guided tour. Tours commence when the students use the mouse to select a coach icon, and they are then guided around a sequence of frames until the tour ends, at which point the student is returned to the starting point. Students can at all times leave the tour to explore other frames, or to consult frames detailing further reading. They can rejoin the tour at their point of departure later. Tours can also incorporate other tours, which we term excursions. The mouse icon is changed to a small coach as an identifier of the tour mode.

The metaphor is extended to encompass the whole range of access facilities. The conventional form of hypertext navigation, through selecting active areas using the mouse, can be termed 'go-it-alone' travel or rambling. We have adopted a convention that any item displayed in yellow denotes a selectable item. To help students find their way around the materials we provide a number of additional tools. Maps permit the student to see where they are in relation to other display frames and also indicate the linkages between frames. Maps can be used to 'orienteer' around the system, as any frame can be selected directly from a map. The maps are dynamic in the sense that they indicate which frame the map was evoked from (a 'You are here' indicator), and also which frames have previously been visited. A typical screen from the 'Cognitive Psychology' module is shown in Fig 2, where each rectangle represents one or more information frames. The selection of any rectangle results in the display of the associated screens. A second tool, the index, is also directly accessible from all information frames. On selection it allows direct access to keyword-coded frames (or tours).

A small number of other facilities are provided which do not form part of the metaphor. The most important of these is the provision of multiple choice quizzes. The questions are related to the current topic, and form not only a method of self-assessment but also a form of navigation. From any multiple choice question, the student has an option of asking for further explanations, and this produces the most relevant frame(s) on the topic area before returning the user to the quiz. When quizzes are used to navigate the information screens, the quiz questions themselves become 'advance organizers', and hence add structure to the learning task.

Evaluation

During the early prototyping of the system, small-scale studies with potential users highlighted several problem areas, ranging from the mouse dialogue and colour usage, to the need for access tools over and above conventional hypertext selection. Students did not always reach their goals, and sometimes were unaware of this. This early testing revealed the need for tours and maps.

The data employed in our present evaluation of the LSE comes from three sources. The system produces a time-stamped performance log for each student - every screen identifier, its type and time of access is recorded. Secondly, students completed a brief questionnaire at the end of each session. Finally, a selected group of students who had used the system extensively were given an extended questionnaire to complete.

Initially, we concentrated our evaluations on the user interface and the role of the metaphor in assisting the user's understanding of the system. We analysed questionnaire responses from 59 undergraduate students using the Cognitive Psychology module, with no training on the system other than the integrated help facilities. For the question 'How easy was the Hitch-Hiker's Guide to use?', a mean of 11 was obtained on a scale 0 (very easy) to 100 (very difficult). To the question 'How successful were you in achieving your aims?' a mean score of 22 was obtained on a scale 0 (very successful) to 100 (completely unsuccessful). Students were also asked for what tasks they had used the system; their responses are given in Table 1.

Reported system usage	% student usage
Browsing	88%
Information search	86%
Revision	51%
Integration with other teaching	32%
Seeking references	10%

Table 1 *Variety of purposes of system use.*
(most students gave several)

These figures, of course, represent a snapshot of usage, and usage will vary in relation to other educational activities.

In order to examine the use of the four main navigation methods, we analysed system-generated logs for 42 students, who had used the system for at least 30 minutes. See results in Table 2.

Navigation method	% students using each method
Hypertext links	100%
Tour	91%
Index	79%
Map	74%.

Table 2 *General usage of facilities by students.*

Whilst these figures are encouraging, it could be that a significant number of users employed only one method of access and used it regardless of its efficiency. Such a phenomenon is not uncommon, and similar effects are observable in novices using text editors (Rosson, 1984). In fact, most methods were used by most students, though often to varying degrees: 57% used all four methods, 29% used three and the remaining 14% used only two methods.

A free-recall test given to 16 students (average use of the system of 85 minutes) at least a week following their most recent session did result in all four methods of access being represented, but the students' breadth of recall did not match their breadth of actual usage. A second part of this test asked what type of access facilities they would use for particular tasks. The results are summarised below.

Task	Most popular	Second most popular
Browsing	Map	Index
Information search	Index	Hypertext
Revision	all equally popular	
Seeking references	Index	Hypertext
Study of unfamiliar material	Tour	Index
Study of partially familiar material	Map	Index
Study of familiar material	Hypertext	Index

Table 3 *Reported use of facilities with respect to user's task.*

It seems that increasing familiarity with the topic results in a shift from system control (ie tours), through shared control (ie maps) to user control (ie hypertext links). This initial study demonstrated that, given a set of access facilities, students use them widely and, certainly in terms of self-reporting, in an appropriate task-directed manner. A more recent study tackles the same general issues but from a different standpoint, namely how is performance affected by limiting the range of access tools. The conclusions from this study is that there are problems with hypertext alone which can be overcome by the use of appropriate navigational tools (Hammond & Allinson, 1989). Techniques for measuring knowledge acquisition and concept formation are also being developed for LSE investigations.

Conclusions

From the studies we have conducted we can conclude that the system is easy to use and that the navigational tools provided were indeed used by the students. Not only were the tools used, but they appeared to be used strategically, in a manner appropriate for the tasks undertaken. These findings are further endorsed in Hammond and Allinson (1989).

We have outlined the philosophy and development of a LSE for non-formal knowledge domains. The need for a variety of access methods has been examined and also borne out by our evaluation of the system in actual use. The provision of a conventional hypertext access is not sufficient in a learning environment when the variable context of the material, needs, user ability and learning strategies are considered.

The Hitch-Hiker's Guide has proved itself to be a successful tool not only as a practical vehicle for providing an LSE both within our university department and outside, but also as a means for investigating the success or otherwise of various navigation tools in providing useful learning facilities. We believe that it is important, wherever possible, to obtain empirical evidence to support the application and precise style of any LSE.

References

Conklin J (1987) Hypertext: an introduction and survey. *IEEE Computer* 20 (9): 17-41.

Entwistle N (1987) A model of the teacher-learning process. In: *Student Learning*. Edited by Richardson J T E, Eysenck M W and Piper D W. Open University Press, Milton Keynes. pp 13-28.

Hammond N V and Allinson L J (1987) The travel metaphor as design principle and training aid for navigating around complex systems. In: *People and Computers III*. Edited by Diaper D and Winder R. Cambridge University Press, Cambridge. pp 75-90.

Hammond N V and Allinson L J (1988) Development and evaluation of a CAL system for non-formal domains: the hitch-hiker's guide to cognition. *Computer Education* 12. pp 215-220.

Hammond N V and Allinson L J (1988) Travels around a learning support environment: rambling, orienteering or touring? In: *CHI '88 Conference Proceedings: Human Factors in Computer Systems*. Edited by Soloway E, Frye D and Sheppard S B. Washington, May. ACM Press, New York. pp 269-273.

Hammond N V and Allinson L J (1989) Extending hypertext for learning: an investigation of access and guidance tools. Paper submitted to CHI '89, Austin, April 1989.

Pask G and Scott B C E (1972) Learning strategies and individual competence. *International Journal of Man-Machine Studies* 4. pp 217-253.

Rosson M B (1984) Effects of experience on learning, using and evaluating a text editor. *Human Factors* 26. pp 463-475.

Notes

[1]   Development of the system was supported by a grant from the Computers in Teaching Initiative (CTI) of the UGC Computer Board.

5

Patricia Baird
Mark Percival

Glasgow online: database development using Apple's HyperCard

Abstract

This chapter examines the problems of creating a hypertext system of community information. Managing the complexity of the system and providing connections throughout to meet the information needs of a broad spectrum of users can only be accomplished by a process of continual tracking during and after development. Several evaluation exercises have been undertaken to assess whether database design, presentation of information, link establishment, etc, are sufficient to meet the needs of the broad spectrum of users which is the target audience of Glasgow Online. There are difficulties in presenting a computer-supported information environment for a variety of users, many of whom are non-computer literate.

What is hypertext?

Hypertext has been described as:

> 'non-sequential reading and writing...allowing authors to link information, create paths through a corpus of related material, annotate existing texts, create notes and point readers to either bibliographical data or the body of the referenced text' (Conklin, 1987)

The concept is one of free-range access to a computer-supported information environment. This is achieved by linking discrete elements in the database thereby setting up a cross-referenced system through which users can navigate in any direction. Hypertexts, therefore, allow users access to non-linear information. There is no one 'right' way to use or access a hypertext. Users navigate the system by means of the links embedded by the author, according to specific user need.

Three major areas of concern arise in the production and use of hypertexts:

1   design and presentation of data which will be both easy to use and easy to understand;

2   determining user need;

3   reading non-linear documents which are devoid of traditional guiding mechanisms.

Glasgow online: HyperCard database

These problems will be illustrated in the context of Glasgow Online, a hypertext system being developed by the Department of Information Science at the University of Strathclyde, using Apple's HyperCard. Glasgow Online will be an integrated database on the life and times of the city of Glasgow. The information is already available albeit in scattered form. The aim of the project is to use the medium of hypertext, not to emulate the many books, pamphlets, guides, etc. on Glasgow, but to integrate, repackage and restructure that information to provide users with an electronic conspectus on the city and its culture. Essentially, therefore, Glasgow Online will be a hypertext of community information. 'Community' is not narrowly defined, but comprises a heterogeneous grouping including tourists, researchers, teachers, students, businessmen, potential inward investors, as well as Glasgow's indigenous population. The database will be a public domain utility and will be given at zero cost to interested agencies and organizations throughout the city and beyond.

Design and presentation of data

A distinction must be drawn (see Garrett *et al*, 1986) between categorization of hypertexts:

single author ——— single reader

single author ——— many readers

many authors ——— many readers

Glasgow Online will be a read-only system in the first instance, and so will not be dynamic in the sense of readers as authors adding to the corpus of material, like the much-documented Xanadu project, on which Ted Nelson has been working since the late sixties. The Glasgow hypertext will be created by a team of authors for a broad and quite distinct spectrum of readers. Presentation of data will be through text and graphics arranged in HyperCard stacks. Access will be mouse-driven. The minimal finding unit will be a word or icon on a card in a stack which, when activated by pointing and clicking the mouse, will transport the user to another place in the hyperdocument. These active areas are known as buttons. The database will initially consist of the sixteen areas shown in Fig 1.

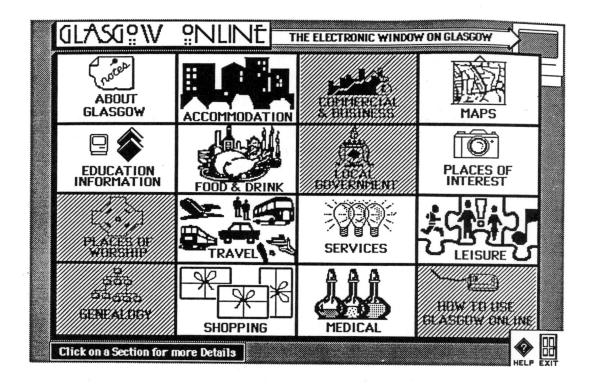

Fig 1 *Initial HyperCard screen*

These areas have not been chosen arbitrarily, but after consultation with a number of bodies who are providing information under the various headings, eg, the Tourist Board, local government departments, shops, businesses, hotels, travel services, relocation agencies, libraries, etc.

The authors' task is to create an environment which will allow multiple pathways, while managing the complexity of the data and not compromising the system. It is expected that Mark 1 of this database will require about 15 megabytes of storage capacity. Information is being gathered, validated, updated and put into the system in such a way that any user can follow any trail to find specific information according to needs and wants. What are the easy to follow, recognizable structures along which the authors must create the links so that users can attain these objectives?

Data structures

Hierarchical structures, in the main, offer both author and reader a recognizable way to proceed. However, links should also be provided which will permit lateral movement and allow the user to follow a non-sequential path. As early as 1945 Vannevar Bush (Meadows,1988) described a virtual device called Memex which resembled a mechanized private file and library:

> *'a device in which an individual stores all his books, records, and communications...an enlarged intimate supplement to his memory'.*

Bush held human mental agility as:

> *'awe-inspiring beyond all else in nature. Man cannot hope fully to duplicate this mental process artificially, but he certainly ought to be able to learn from it'.*

The author's task has been described (Hardman, 1988) along lines of mental association. The author has a particular 'chunk' of information he wishes to communicate to the reader. This information exists in the author's head as a network of related points. John Smith (Smith, 1987) describes the funnelling process the author goes through in order to construct a linear document. For a hypertext the author is not obliged to cut out all the network links to form a strict hierarchy and then lay out the hierarchy in a linear form. Instead, the information can be put into the hypertext in the same structure as it is in the author's head.

It would be foolish to suppose that all the nodes in the Glasgow Online system could or should be linked. This would neither be helpful to the user whose chances of getting lost in the hyperdocument would increase, nor to the authors who have to manage the complexity of the data; nor could the system support channels of communication to this extent and still function effectively. But, as Bush suggested, we can learn from the web of associations represented by the complex interconnection of brain cells, the speed with which these connections are made and paths are followed. Authors, therefore, have to consider models for structuring data and ways of identifying data to be linked other than adherence to hierarchical principles.

Models

Glasgow Online is considering an amalgamation of various models:

- the guided tour along hierarchical lines with the author in control;

- a system of explicit signalling which links items non-hierarchically and allows preferred, though controlled, navigation through the data;

- 'subliminal' signalling, eg, underlined, highlighted, italicized type which the user is electronically nudged to follow. The user feels more in control, yet the author has still selected and laid down possible routes.

- choosing from the array of metaphors which abound in the discussion of hypertexts and providing users with maps or browsers.

Metaphors

The analogy of hypertext mapping to topographical maps is very important. Work at Edinburgh University's department of Psychology suggests that users construct a cognitive representation of hypertext structures in the form of a survey map (Edwards, 1988). The author also concludes that one of the most common metaphors, the electronic book, is an appropriate format for hypertext information systems. Comparisons and analogies between the virtual world of the hyperdocument and the real world of everyday experience allow users to construct a more accurate mental model of what to expect from the hypertext. Work in this field supports the idea that metaphors in general, and the travel metaphor in particular, are extremely powerful aids to navigation around complex data structures such as hypertext systems. Other metaphors in the context of the Glasgow system, such as an Architectural Walk, an Historical Journey, the Educational Arena, Shopping Basket, Discovering Business Opportunities, etc will contribute to the user's expectations of what the system has to offer.

A metaphor not only helps the non-expert user, but also forms a relatively rigid framework within which the author must work to maintain consistency. The value of the metaphor can be seen by a comparison between a standard IBM PC/MS DOS interface (without the GEM or Windows environment) and an Apple Macintosh interface. The former relies entirely on command lines for operation while the latter makes extensive use of such metaphors as document, desktop, clipboard, files, waste basket, etc. The metaphorical environment of the Macintosh interface increases comprehension and is considered easier to use.

Hammond and Allison (Hammond and Allison, 1987) review the effectiveness of various metaphors and how they affect cognition, concluding that there is a danger that metaphors can become too restrictive:

> 'the system should improve upon the metaphor, not be bounded by it. A metaphor can support partial mappings of knowledge with no ambiguity provided it is well chosen and provided the system is designed appropriately around it.'

Of course, whatever the nature of the metaphor, it will have physical restrictions. Users of Glasgow Online will enjoy and benefit from an Architectural Walk around the city, but miss out on the physical sensations. Moving into a hypermedia environment where the user can extend the system to access external devices such as interactive videodisc players, online information services, CD-ROM drives, VCRs and so on, could go some way to remedy that. The department is already holding discussions to move Mark 2 of the database into hypermedia.

User interface: design factors

One of the guiding principles in this area is to match interface design to user needs. Input from experienced graphic designers to hypertext systems has not figured prominently, in spite of the extensive graphics capabilities of some packages. The effectiveness of graphics in communicating information has been examined by Kindborg and Kollerbaur, who believe that the graphic dynamism of comic books, with their sophisticated interweaving of text and pictures, may point the way to the development of more visually attractive and effective user interfaces (Kindborg and Kollerbaur,1987). Frequently, interactive systems do not exploit more than a fraction of the graphics power that is available, and few are influenced by the rules and principles governing presentation of graphic material in printed form. Related problems that arise most often in interactive systems include unclear status information, failure to show process status, and misinterpreted icons. Another important point is that motion strongly attracts attention. If animation, however simple, can be included in a system, it immediately becomes more attractive. Figs 2 and 3 indicate the extent of graphics use in Glasgow Online.

Process visualization

It is vital, especially for the novice user, to have some idea of what is going on in a system after a particular process has been set in motion. This is called process visualization and in its simplest form can be seen in the Macintosh interface when an icon expands into a window as a folder or document is opened. If any time at all is to elapse during the process, the user should always be made aware that something is happening, and that no user error has occurred. The clock icon which appears whilst information is being processed by the Macintosh is a simple yet most effective example of process visualisation. Kindborg and Kollerbaur conclude:

> 'It is vitally important to include professional media experts and professional communicators in the design process'.

Unfortunately, this is something that has not been a major consideration in the design of many hypertext packages and applications. There has to be greater involvement of people skilled in the art of design and communication otherwise hypertext systems will continue to fall short of their potential as radically new

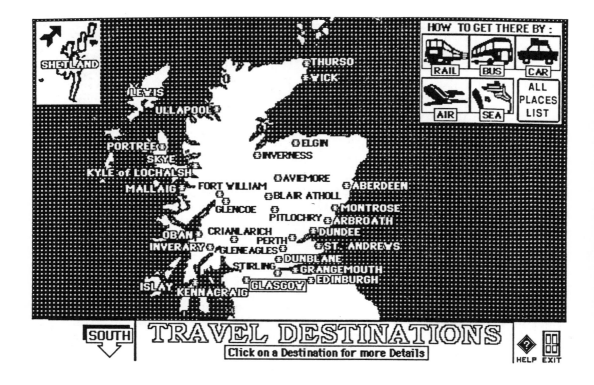

Fig 2 *Travel destinations*

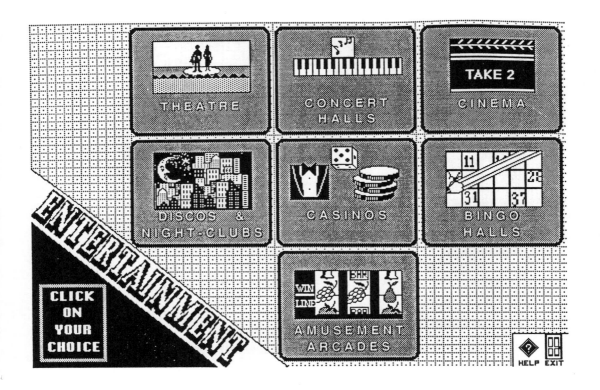

Fig 3 *Entertainment*

ways of presenting and disseminating information. Much has been written about HyperCard since its launch in 1987. Apple's decision to distribute HyperCard with every new Macintosh may well have a profound effect on the development of user interface design and user awareness of hypertext systems. It was partly for its superb graphics capabilities that HyperCard was chosen as the vehicle for Glasgow Online. Graphics are extremely important when the intended users of the system are likely to be non- computer-literate members of the general public whose information needs are not catered for by existing electronic services. As Nelson notes:

> 'Today's conventional databases will not satisfy the information needs of the non-computing public, nor can they provide methods for publishing the ever-more-interconnected writings now placed on electronic networks.' (Nelson, 1988).

Determining user need

Looking at existing models and following metaphors can assist authors in the design and presentation of data in hypertext systems. Information is sterile, however, without use and it is only by examining how readers use the system, that we, as authors, can assess whether the presentation of data and establishment of links is sufficient to meet user needs. The spectrum of cognitive activity in a system designed to meet community information requirements matches the spectrum of users. It is impossible to meet every need that every user will bring to the database. For the authors of such systems, the logistics of presenting non-linear information to meet a variety of cognitive styles is considerable. In the case of Glasgow Online, several evaluation exercises have been set in motion to track and monitor patterns of use during (and after) development of Mark1 of the database. The results, in each case, will be used to refine the database. Evaluation exercises have centred on:

- two groups of graduate students;
- an external user group of public and private sector organizations;
- on-site evaluation at various 'live' situations, eg the Tourist Information Centre, British Airways shuttle lounge at Glasgow Airport, the foyer of the Mitchell Library (Glasgow's main reference library) and the lobby of one of the city's major hotels;
- visitors to the Glasgow Garden Festival;
- a Scottish HCI team from Heriot-Watt University which has recently carried out the first full system evaluation;
- participants at an international conference on industrial mathematics;
- an IT conversion course in the university course for women returning to work;

The first three of these exercises are ongoing and will be reported in due course. Analysis of data collected from items 4 and 5 has been documented elsewhere (Baird *et al*, 1988). The two remaining produced some interesting factors.

Questionnaire results

The evaluation exercises were conducted using a structured questionnaire which followed established guidelines for measuring user interface satisfaction and was designed for a broad spectrum of users. It is generally recognized that speed and accuracy are two related factors which affect user attitude towards systems. Learning time and ease of recall are also important. Above all, it is critical that the user accepts and is satisfied with the system if system utility is to be maximized. The questionnaire was necessarily brief. Users were asked to answer questions on a scale of seven points. It should be stressed that the questionnaire was designed to gather as much rough quantitative data as quickly and efficiently as possible. So while it is not exhaustive, it is the optimum length for obtaining the required quality of information.

Twenty three questions were gathered into five groups:

- first impressions of the system;

- clarity and organization of information on screen;

- terminology and system information;

- learning from the system;

- speed and ease of use.

ECMI

Group Six comprised participants at the Second European Conference of Mathematicians in Industry (ECMI) which was held in the University during the summer of 1988. This occasion provided a valuable opportunity to demonstrate the system to one of the most likely eventual user groups - visitors to the city. Equally important was the fact that for many, English was not their first language. Any complicated text or ambiguous icon/graphic interpretations would be highlighted more quickly.

Many of the ECMI participants used the system for specific searches and they were, therefore, the first real users of Glasgow Online looking for restaurants, bars, sports facilities, places of interest and other tourist attractions. Initial (qualitative) observations indicated positive response from those using the system and also from those ECMI participants observing.

Wider opportunities for women course

Group Seven consisted of twenty-two women attending a ten week course run by the University which aims to enhance the future employment prospects of women returning to work by increasing their awareness of, and giving them experience of, Information Technology and related applications. This group was broadly non-computer literate and, as such, formed a useful contrast to the mathematicians.

Results

Twenty-eight questionnaires were returned by the ECMI users from a total conference attendance of 153 - 18.3%. Twenty-two were returned from the women's group - 100% of the course attendees for that day. For the purposes of this survey, the responses of the two groups will be compared. There are clear differences between the two groups.

Tables 1, 2 and 3 graphically display the results. Comparing the two groups indicates that Group Seven rated every question higher than group 6 except one question which asked how hard the characters were to read on screen (reasons for this will be discussed later). The most significant result to emerge from the survey was that there were very few individual ratings below the median of three. So reaction to the system has been almost entirely positive as an overview of the results of the questionnaire will show.

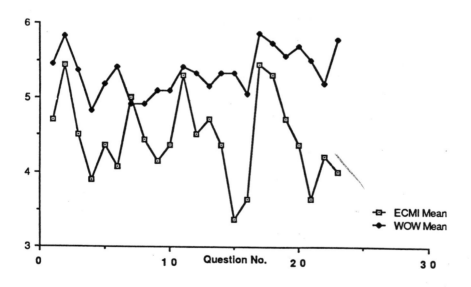

Table 1 *Comparison of mean results*

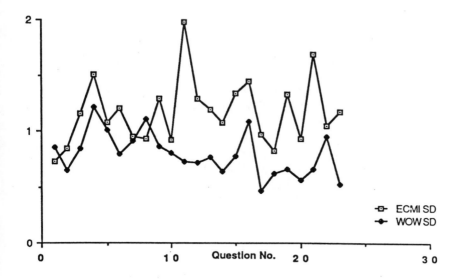

Table 2 *Comparison of standard deviations*

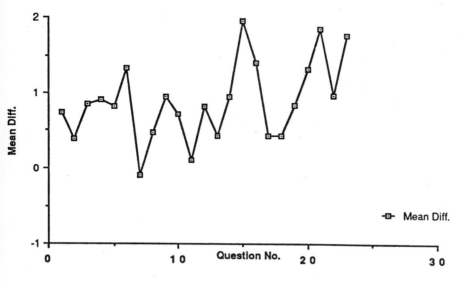

Table 3 *Mean difference for questions*

Computer literacy

The only major difference between the two groups lies in their degree of computer literacy. The mix of ages was roughly similar and the fact that Group Seven consisted only of women seems relatively unimportant. The computer-literate mathematicians rated the system lower than the novice users. The former knew what to expect from the computer while the agility of the personal computer, especially one as relatively powerful as a Mac SE, was almost entirely new and all the more impressive to the women's group. The following section extracts the major findings of the survey under the group headings. A fuller account has been documented elsewhere (Percival, 1988).

First impressions

Both groups thought the system could be more powerful in some way - better information retrieval facilities or faster link transactions. Expectations, of course, were of a different order.

Clarity

In the second category on clarity and organization of the system, one question (and the only one in the questionnaire) was rated lower by the women's group. This question (alluded to above, on ease of reading on screen) received a higher rating from the ECMI group who are familiar with reading from a computer screen, whereas the women's group had little experience at reading computer monitors, especially the relatively small screen of the Mac SE.

Terminology/system information

The largest mean difference between the two groups was a question in Section 3 on how the system kept users informed about what it was doing (process visualization capabilities). This question not only scored the lowest mean result, but also the largest mean difference between the two groups. The ECMI group was generally familiar with standard Macintosh processing signals, eg the watch or the beachball. The present version of Glasgow Online has not yet included process signals at present, and this can lead to too many mouse-clicks and subsequent errors in activated links. Novices do not expect to find process indicators, so the results from Group Seven for that question reflect the users' overall positive attitude to the system rather than the answer to that specific question.

Learning

Both groups produced some of the highest scores in the section on learning. They considered the system very easy to learn to use, with a relatively small mean difference.

System capabilities

The last section produced the second highest score from Group Seven and also one of the largest mean differences between the two groups. It seems that experienced users do not quite understand the needs of the inexperienced user. As people become more accustomed to using computers, they seem to change their perceptions of themselves and other users to the extent that they forget what it was like when they first faced a VDU. As is now becoming clear, computer-literacy is the deciding factor in the results of this survey.

A more predictable result occurred in the question about system speed. The ECMI group was obviously used to much faster hard and software. None of them, however, had encountered a hypertext system previously and they had no fixed preconceptions on what to expect from HyperCard or Glasgow Online.

Further significant factors

Various comments were made in addition to the questionnaire, some of which should be mentioned. Users were generally unhappy about the mouse as the system pointer. The developers of Glasgow Online are actively considering alternative devices for moving the on-screen pointer, eg a joystick, roller-ball or touch screen. As with other users of the system (see Baird *et al*, 1988) some members of these user groups experienced difficulty with the 'Exit' icon (a door) wishing it to be larger and its function made more clear. Universally, users wish the button areas on screen to have a clearer definition. Often they found them difficult to pinpoint. The colour version of HyperCard, which Apple expect to release in mid-89, should greatly assist. Most users felt that although the small monochrome screen was reasonably easy to become accustomed to, it is not attractive at first glance and therefore may run the risk of being ignored by potential users in a real-world situation.

Future evaluation

The survey described above has been a very useful first step towards amassing quantitative data on user reaction to Glasgow Online. It is, however, merely the tip of the evaluation iceberg. As more data is obtained from a larger sample of the potential user group, more appropriate and comprehensive methods of assessing the system will emerge. It is also intended to incorporate a system of extended tracking-in-use by placing counters on cards. In particular, this data (though by no means conclusive since there is no way of tracking user error nor establishing whether or not a search has been successful) will indicate levels of use of specific cards, which cards are being accessed from particular buttons, how often users return to the home card and perhaps most important of all, which cards are not used at all.

Reading non-linear text

An interesting account of problems encountered when reading non-linear text was presented during the1987 HyperText conference held in North Carolina (Charney, 1987). In the absence of traditional 'cues and clues' readers have a tendency to gain little from the hyperdocument and often get lost. It is vital, therefore, that the system incorporates step-back mechanisms, and means of mapping which will allow recovery. Glasgow Online has much to offer in the way of satisfying community information needs but, because of the amount and the complexity of the information, it has to be monitored very carefully. The extent of the problem of satisfying a variety of cognitive needs while managing and manipulating large-scale storage of information is considerable. However, it is generally reckoned that hypertext and hypermedia, because of their general applicability, will have a big impact on the world of end-user computing in the near future. Glasgow Online could be part of this predicted surge of interest.

References

Baird P, Mac Morrow N and Hardman L (1988) Cognitive aspects of constructing non-linear documents: HyperCard and Glasgow Online. Online Information 88, *Proceedings of 12th International Online Information Meeting*, Olympia 2, London.

Charney D (1987) Comprehending non-linear text: the role of discourse cues and reading strategies. *Proceedings of HyperTEXT '87*, North Carolina. pp 109-119.

Conklin J (1987) Hypertext: an introduction and survey. *IEEE Computer* 20 (9): 17-41.

Edwards D M (1988) Lost in hyperspace: cognitive mapping and navigation in a hypertext environment. Unpublished thesis. University of Edinburgh.

Garrett N, Smith K E and Meyrowitz N (1986) Intermedia: issues, strategies and tactics in the design of a hypermedia document system. *Proceedings of the conference on computer-supported cooperative work*, Austin, Texas. pp 163-174.

Hammond N V and Allinson L J (1987) The travel metaphor as design principle and training aid for navigating around complex systems. In: *People and Computers III*. Edited by Diaper D and Winder R. Cambridge University Presss, Cambridge. pp 75-90.

Hardman L (1988) Hypertext tips: experiences in developing a hypertext tutorial. *Proceedings of HCI Conference*, Cambridge.

Kindborg M and Kollerbaur A (1987) Visual languages and human computer interaction. *People and computers III*. Edited by Diaper D and Winder R. Cambridge University Press, Cambridge. pp 176-187.

Meadows J (Editor) (1988) *The Origins of Information Science*. London.

Nelson T H (1988) Managing immense storage. *Byte*. pp 225-238.

Percival M (1988) Hypertext, Hypermedia and HyperCard: a critical review of cognitive and design aspects and an evaluation of Glasgow Online. Unpublished thesis, University of Strathclyde.

Smith J (1987) A hypertext writing environment and its cognitive basis. *Proceedings of HyperTEXT '87*, North Carolina. pp 195-214.

6

Phil Cooke
Ian Williams
Design issues in large hypertext systems for technical documentation

Abstract
With the advent of commercial hypertext software products, designers are addressing the problems of adapting this new technology to complex documentation systems. The challenge is twofold: to extend the hypertext technology so that it meets user needs in a variety of contexts and to integrate the technology with conventional paper-based systems. Rather than address the related design issues from a theoretical viewpoint, this paper reflects recent experience in developing several complex systems for the engineering industry.

Guide™ hypertext
The term 'hypertext' was coined by Ted Nelson in 1965, but Nelson attributes the underlying concepts to Vannevar Bush who presented his ideas in a classic article on Memex (Bush, 1945).

A number of experimental systems have been developed. Douglas Englebart's Memex-like NLS implementation at Stanford is also known for the introduction of the mouse, multiple windows, and other innovations familiar to workstation users. Xerox PARC have developed a system called Notecards. In addition to Nelson's ambitious Xanadu project (Nelson, 1981), there is Intermedia at Brown University (Meyrowitz, 1986), and Guide at the University of Kent (Brown, 1986).

The work on Guide by Peter Brown led in 1986 to the first commercial implementation of a hypertext system by Office Workstations Limited - first on Apple Macintosh, and then on IBM and compatible computers. Apple computer themselves have recently released a product called HyperCard, which is quite similar to Xerox Notecards, and it seems likely that the number of commercial implementations will increase.

The basic design goal of hypertext software is that users should be able to explore information freely, in multiple parallel paths, instead of being confined to a fixed path or structure.

Guide™ can be described as a system in which the reader is provided with a friendly interface to screen-based documentation. Guide does not attempt to imitate the linear structures of paper-based information. Rather it presents a hierarchical view of information, allowing the user to read only those parts of the documents in which he is interested. The reader simply points to a text highlight (called a button) with a mouse-driven cursor, clicks the mouse and displays a detailed expansion. In addition to text, Guide supports high resolution graphics, and graphical objects can also be made into buttons. Similar point/click actions on other types of button cause reference points in the same document or in other documents to be displayed, or cause pop-up notes to appear. Navigation within and between documents is simple and intuitive. Another important feature of the software is that the author's view of documents is identical to that of the reader.

Requirements of technical documentation systems

Although Guide was initially developed as a retail product for single users, its applicability to documentation was recognized at an early stage. A number of systems based on it have been designed for application to large technical documentation systems in the engineering industry. These systems are quite diverse and include CD-ROM based manuals for automotive repair and catalogues of car parts, standards documents for design and production engineering in the aviation industry, the production of user documentation by computer manufacturers and operation and maintenance manuals in nuclear power generation.

Despite the diversity of these applications, there are a number of requirements which are common to all the systems described. There are significant differences in the design problems posed by networks on the one hand and CD-ROM based systems on the other. For the most part this paper refers to network implementations, though there are very close similarities in both cases, especially in the requirements of authors.

The outstanding feature of all these applications is that the number of documents is very large. The very size of these collections requires the provision of tools which technical authors can use to manage the collection prior to publication. Readers require help to find the documents they wish to consult.

This has led to the design of a shell environment known as Idex, incorporating a Document Manager, and supporting a number of processes:

- Document conversion

- Indexing and retrieval

- Document style management

and features:

- Tables of contents

- Lists of illustrations

- System glossaries and bibliographies
- Help facilities

in addition to those basic applications needed to author and read documents.

System organization

The general structure of Idex is layered, such that we can readily substitute comparable processes for those implemented as standard features. For example, there is no difficulty installing entirely different printing or retrieval engines. Small changes in the user interface, and the replacement of an interpreter are all that is required.

This is an important feature when the need for connectivity to other systems is so obvious. So is the use of a standard network product, which we expect to be directly replaced with enhanced functionality by OS/2 LAN resources.

Use of standards

Adherence to a number of standards can bring long term benefits. Idex has been designed around three important standards relating to networks, database access, and user interface.

Large collections of documents can be shared quite efficiently over a local area network in which a host computer supports a file server containing a document store. A typical configuration includes a DEC VAX host running VMS services for MS-DOS or a similar implementation of MS-Net. IBM-PC/ATs or compatible microcomputers are connected to the network over an Ethernet, and run the hypertext process locally.

The initial version of Idex has been built around a proprietary database. However, the intention has always been to adopt a standard access method which leaves a great deal of independence as regards the nature of the database being used to catalogue the document collection. SQL appears to be the best candidate in this area with opportunities for unifying support for database access mechanisms and networking solutions with the advent of OS/2.

Running as it does under Microsoft Windows version 2, Idex benefits from the tools that the environment provides towards adherence to the Systems Application Architecture (SAA) standard. It also ensures a smooth migration to OS/2 systems in the near future.

The document collection

In theory there can be many document collections in a system, but thus far in practice the design has set a single collection at the top level. Each collection is associated with a single MS-DOS volume.

Document type

The next level of organization is associated with the concept of document type. Document type is user defined and can be any convenient system of classification, such as design standard, specification, production tool drawing, operation flow chart, parts list, etc.

Typing determines a variety of attributes, including how a document is indexed, and how it is styled on the screen display or how it appears if it is printed. The document manager creates a directory for each type and its associated style files. Those of you who have used MS-DOS will know how unhelpful the filename and pathname conventions can be. The task of keeping track of this unwieldy nomenclature, and of such things as unique document references is handled by the Document Manager. The user sees only full document titles.

Document status

Document status (draft, approved, issued, etc), describes the stage reached in the document 'life cycle' and is used to control the publication process and (with other controls) to limit user access privileges. The Document Manager application provides a formalized mechanism for changes in document status allowing full control of the progress of a document towards publication. Draft documents can be edited by authors and read by editors. Only approved documents can be issued and only issued documents can be viewed by readers.

Catalogue card

Because documents are maintained in a database they can be represented to users of the system in terms of their attributes, including document status described above. These attributes are shown through a Catalogue Card interface, familiar to the vast majority of users. Each Catalogue Card can be brought into view when the appropriate document is being browsed.

Application structure

As stated above, the structure of the Idex applications is layered with an Indexer module providing services to the calling application whether this be the reader, author or Document Manager. This allows a consistency of interface across the whole application suite. In addition, the structure of the Indexer module allows all other applications in the suite to call on the hypertext component to present related information, whether this is online help, example material or any other context-sensitive information.

Finding documents

In keeping with the design goal of providing a variety of paths through the collection there should be several ways of finding documents. Most users of technical documents know their system well and clearly prefer to use conventional access paths such as tables of contents and lists of illustrations. At shell level there may be a number of contents tables which consist largely of reference buttons linked to documents concerned. Clicking on the button opens the required document.

In some cases it is useful for a reader to search for a subset of documents defined by criteria like document type, subject, or date. This is implemented by creating an entry for each document in a file of 'catalogue cards'. Cards for different document types can contain appropriate field combinations, thus allowing, for example, a design standard to be indexed by part number and a drawing by scale, while sharing common fields such as author and issue number.

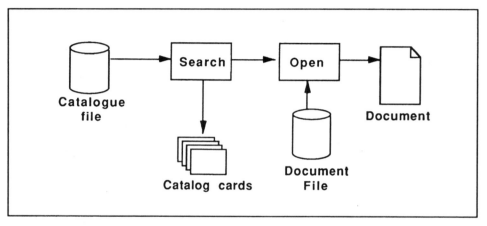

Fig 1 *A search of the catalogue first produces a 'hit list' of cards - the user then opens the required document.*

Selected fields in the cards are inverted in a multikey index. The user can search the indexes by writing search scripts with a context-sensitive editor and can name and save commonly used scripts.

The output of the search process is either a filtered list of document titles which can be displayed in a list box in an 'open' dialogue or a view of the catalogue cards (Fig 1). The results of such searches can be combined into Worklists which can also be saved for future reference. Thus useful sets of documents can be presented to the more naive users of the system - typically the readers - removing them entirely from the complexities of the search process. Search formats can also be saved for convenience.

Maintaining house style

For any publishing organization a consistent house style is very important. Layout and typography are valuable signposts to readers. Screen-based documentation is no exception to this rule.

On screen

We have found that hypertext structure can be used somewhat like generalized markup. Information required for screen display, typographical style, indentation, window size and position, etc is stored at shell level. Consistency across sets of documents is maintained by editing style files for each document type. As a document is displayed the application refers to the style file for the necessary display parameters. This approach allows both the distinctive styling of documents which the authors wish to appear different and the easy modification of style by accessing a single display template.

In print

Because there will always be internal and external users who do not have access to terminals, printed versions of the hypertext documents are required. Naturally enough an identical approach to that used to style screen display has been used for printed output, where each document type has a page layout, and print style templates.

The Page Template Editor accessed through the Document Manager allows the user to lay out the format of the printed page, not only the position of the area to receive document text and graphics, but also static information such as the document title, page number, and any Catalogue Card attribute. These areas are formatted on demand during the printing process.

Despite the good quality of fonts now available for high resolution screens, it is clear that fonts that are easy to read on the screen are not the best for printed text. Unfortunately new fonts designed to meet the needs of both media, like Lucida, are not yet commercially available (Bigelow and Holmes, 1986). The solution is usually to totally restyle the document for print.

Shell documents and functions

Shell documents have document types like any other. They have special purposes however, such as holding contents information, lists of illustrations, a bibliography and a glossary. The use of contents tables and of lists of illustrations has been mentioned above and the others deserve a brief mention.

The bibliography contains descriptions of documents outside the hypertext collection. Citations in other documents point to individual entries and are linked like any other cross-reference. Each entry can contain structure allowing the reader to obtain more detail about a title by expanding the document.

Glossaries contain the definitions of note buttons in documents. However, the definitions are global to the collection as distinct from those that are local to an individual document. Like local definitions, glossaries can contain both text and graphics.

An important category are the Help files. It is appropriate for a hypertext system to be self-documenting. Help documents may contain internal indexes which allow context-sensitivity to be provided to any application in the Idex suite.

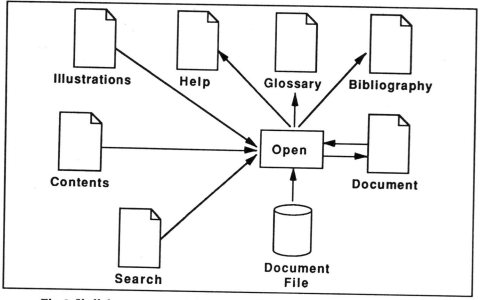

Fig 2 *Shell documents contain buttons that initiate Open actions on other documents in the collection.*

Context messages are passed by any relevant application to the Indexer module and are used to find a specific point in the Help file when help is invoked by the user.

There is also a special, hidden hypertext document at shell level. In it authors can name and save fragments of hypertext structure which can be combined in new, arbitrarily complex structures in any other document. They have proved to be invaluable in the repetitive construction of such structures as flow charts, and complex graphics. If required, structure templates for entire documents can be stored in this way.

Document conversion

A major task facing the authors of a hypertext system is the creation of structured documents and it therefore seemed important that we should build tools that could simplify this process.

Text

In most cases existing documents contain some accessible text structure. If the documents exist in machine-readable form they usually contain embedded markup used by the word processor on which they were prepared or, more rarely, full encoding in a general markup language like SGML(ISO86).

If no machine-readable version is available, there are alternatives. With typeset texts, scanning devices using intelligent character recognition techniques can be used to substitute the markup implied by the typographic content. The same scanners can even make sense of poor quality typescript which has been photocopied several times over. From a file containing suitable markup we can now create structure for a hypertext document containing at least a hierarchy of headings, in the worst case by parsing section and sub-section numbers. However, a richly encoded source document leads to a more satisfactory conversion process. In addition to hierarchy, cross-references (including forward references) and notes can be linked to their target structures.

Owing to the wide variety of source encoding expected, a two-stage process has been chosen. First a source document is converted to a closely specified intermediate format by any convenient utility. The user then maps the intermediate format to hypertext structure and runs the second part of the conversion procedure.

Graphics

As well as providing tools for processing existing text files, we have had some success with the conversion of graphics. Data in vector format poses few problems, and usually some simple text editing tools are all that is required. We are looking forward to the day when the MS-Windows metafile format will support hierarchical graphic structures, enabling hypertext structure to be applied to imported drawings.

Dealing with bitmaps is less straightforward. First of all, with bitmaps that are already digitized, conversion from one resolution to another is usually less that satisfactory. Also, there is a significant difference between the resolution required for screen display of bitmaps (70-100 dpi) than that required if documents in the system are to be printed on laser printers (300 dpi). In some cases the solution has been to rescan the images and hold the data at both resolutions. Large bitmaps can also prove too large for satisfactory display on smaller screens. As a result graphics editing tools have been developed which make it possible to clean up, segment, and label bitmap images.

CD-ROM variations

The early acceptance of an industry-standard solution for CD-ROM (the High Sierra data format) has made it possible for publishers to issue documents on optical discs in the certainty that users of the information can use devices from a wide range of manufacturers. Up to 550Mb of data can be distributed on a single disk at a very low cost, especially if there are a large number of users.

Since data transfer rates from CD-ROM are rather slow, it makes sense to have document index structures that are optimized for such systems, or to use an external system to address the disk. In the first case our approach has been to work with established retrieval mechanisms developed by third parties. An interesting example of the second case is in a service bay diagnostics system built for Ford

Motor Corporation. The implementation is for a Hewlett Packard Vectra computer. The system provides for a connection to an on-board diagnostic computer in a vehicle. Expert system technology provides diagnostic support and is linked to the documentation, largely held on CD-ROM. This information is supplemented from a remote database connected to the diagnostic system over a dial-up circuit. The expert system contains embedded references to CD-ROM-based hypertext documents, which can also be accessed through tables of contents as described earlier. If the user wishes to read documents held on the database, they are converted to hypertext format at runtime by routines similar to those used for batch process text file conversion. The interface to the three subsystems is designed to be transparent. A simple combination of pointing and scrolling allows the user to select a mode and a subset of documents. Regardless of the source format, documents are displayed in a consistent manner.

One of the more interesting interface modifications for this diagnostic system is the replacement of the cursor/mouse interface with one for use with a touch screen. Service mechanics are generally unfamiliar with computers and there is no scope in the service bay environment for a mouse and keyboard. The constraints of the touch screen display made it necessary to confine display to a single document at a time, to widen the scroll bars, and to replace menu commands with action buttons.

Conclusions

Large, screen-based documentation systems demand innovative designs which are consistent with the overall design goals of hypertext software. The solutions are not immediately obvious since there are few useful precedents from the world of paper-based documentation. Authors are engaged with the problems of how best to present information clearly, concisely and attractively. They need powerful tools that ease the task of converting existing documents to new formats and which enable the management of the entire system. Hypertext systems have been applied in a variety of documentation applications and some common design problems have emerged. We believe that in a relatively short time it will be possible to offer generic tools which can be used with confidence by designers wishing to make the best use of this exciting new technology.

References

Bigelow C and Holmes K (1986) The design of Lucida: an integrated family of types for electronic literacy. In: *Text Processing and Document Manipulation*. Cambridge.

Brown P J (1986) A simple mechanism for authorship of dynamic documents. In: *Text Processing and Document Manipulation*. Cambridge.

Bush V (1945) As we may think. *Atlantic Monthly* 176. pp 101-108.

ISO 8879 (1986) Standard Generalized Markup Language (SGML). Geneva.
Meyrowitz N (1986) The architecture and construction of an object- oriented hypermedia system and applications framework. *OOPSLA '86 Conference Proceedings*, New York.
Nelson T (1981) *Literary Machines*. San Antonio, Texas.

7

Deborah M Edwards
Lynda Hardman

'Lost in hyperspace': cognitive mapping and navigation in a hypertext environment

Abstract

This chapter describes an experiment which looks at how readers of a hypertext cognitively represent its structure. A database of information was formed into three different hypertext structures and presented to readers who answered a series of questions about the information contained in the hypertext. The way the readers found the answers to the questions and how they laid out a representation of the hypertext structure was recorded. Evidence gained from this data points to the formation of a spatial cognitive map by readers, which has implications for the structure of a hypertext and the types of navigation tools that should be provided.

Problems with hypertext

Despite the great enthusiasm with which hypertext packages have been produced, there are still several problems to be overcome. According to Conklin (1987), one of the major problems of hypertext, and the one to which this paper addresses itself, is that of disorientation or 'getting lost' in a display network. Elm and Woods (1985) describe this situation as:

> 'The user not having a clear conception of the relationships within the system, or knowing his present location in the system relative to the display structure, and finding it difficult to decide where to look next within the system'.

They see this disorientation in terms of degradation of user performance rather than a subjective feeling of being 'lost' and define good spatial navigation skills as:

- the ability to generate specific routes as task demands require;

- the ability to traverse or generate new routes as skillfully as familiar ones;

- orientation abilities - the development of a concept of 'here' in relation to other places.

The first two items would be sufficient for a reader to navigate effectively through a hypertext. The third item may or may not be necessary, since all that is required to access a particular piece of information is the appropriate set of links to be actioned from the current location. However, perhaps users are attempting to create a comprehensive cognitive spatial map (a cognitive representation, similar in form to a street plan) of the data structure, complete with locations and routes, or perhaps they represent the environment by means of sequences of actions to each location. Mahony (1988) appears to support the spatial metaphor by suggesting that users would not be disorientated if they had a conceptual overview (or spatial representation) of the structure of the hypertext, stating that:

> 'The main disadvantages of using hypertext at present seem to be consequent of its sheer lack of physical presence and integrity...the very flexibility of reading on screen is disorientating for a user who can't conceptualize an overview of the structure'.

In comparing hypertext with conventional linear text in book form, Conklin (1987) notes that any piece of text that the user wishes to locate in a book can only be further forward or further back from where they are currently located. He reminds us that hypertext, as well as providing us with more locations in which to store information and more dimensions in which to travel, also provides us with greater potential for becoming disorientated or lost. Clearly, locating text if the user doesn't know what is available or how to access it, is a major problem. Jones (1987) points out that in many systems locating screens of information may not be possible without considerable knowledge of the hypertext structure and the user's current position within it. Again comparing hypertext with conventional linear text, Charney (1987) points out that the ordering of topics and points and various traditional orientating devices such as overviews and summaries that are usually taken for granted in books and papers, are non-existent in hypertext, and thus the overall structure of the document is quite different.

These issues raise a number of questions. Is knowledge of the document's structure as important as Jones suggests? Is there any attempt to represent the structure of the document cognitively, and if so, what form does it take?

Cognitive mapping

Several experiments have examined navigation and cognitive mapping in subjects experiencing a new, large-scale physical environment such as a town or city. The most notable of these was by Siegel and White (1975) who proposed a developmental sequence of cognitive representation whereby an individual's knowledge of the environment alters in form through a series of four stages, with each new form being superior to the last. They proposed that subjects initially recognized landmarks, these being objects that for some reason were prominent or notable in the environment, then formed route maps consisting of routes connecting the landmarks, followed by the creation of 'minimaps', which are survey-type maps of small areas, and finally developed full survey maps of the whole area by joining these minimaps together.

Many cognitive mapping studies have examined naturalistic environments, but others have used a simulated environment presented to subjects in the form of a series of slides, eg. Cohen and Schuepfer (1980). Their study examined both route learning through a series of very similar corridors, and the formation of mental survey maps of the layout of the corridors. This form of presentation is very similar to the way in which screens of information in a hypertext database are presented. When subjects are required to access a particular piece of information in hypertext, the screens of data are analogous to rooms or landmarks, and the mouse clicks are analogous to traversing corridors between those screens. Canter, Rivers and Storrs (1985) have also considered the analogy between data navigation and physical environment navigation stating that:

> 'It is fruitful to recognize the direct parallells between navigating concrete environments, such as cities or buildings, and navigating data. After all, such parallells are implicit in the navigation metaphor, so it is worth establishing whether or not there is a fruitful analogy between the psychological processes involved'.

There are two major advantages to having a survey-type cognitive map of any environment, be it a city or a database. Firstly, there is the opportunity to work out and utilize short-cuts to reach desired locations. Secondly, and probably more importantly, if the user/traveller is somehow distracted and/or becomes lost en route, there is a far greater chance that they can regain their bearings and reach their intended destination if they have a spatial cognitive map of the environment than if their knowledge is simply in route form.

Given the advantages of survey-type cognitive maps, and the analogy between navigating in a physical environment and in a hypertext, it seems plausible that the spatial cognitive representation of a hypertext would occur.

Experimental rationale

In order to determine how individuals cognitively represent a database environment in the form of a hypertext document, an experiment was constructed that examined the effects of different hypertext structures on user's perceptions of the document. The hypertext document used for the purpose of the experiment was a specially constructed database containing information about various facilities offered by the City of Edinburgh and Edinburgh University in the form of a public information system. The information in the database was identical for all three conditions of the experiment, the only differences being in the underlying structures of the documents and consequently the methods of exploring the contents available to the subjects. Discussion of the three conditions follows.

Hierarchy condition

The hypertext document had a purely hierarchical structure and could only be explored by means of traversing the hierarchy. See Fig 1.

Mixed condition

Again this had a hierarchical structure, but also had an alphabetical index containing the titles of every screen in the database. The index titles could be actioned to take the user to any screen directly and there was an index link at the foot of every screen in the database, making every screen accessible, via the index, from every other screen. Therefore, users could either traverse the hierarchy or use the index. See Figs 2 and 3.

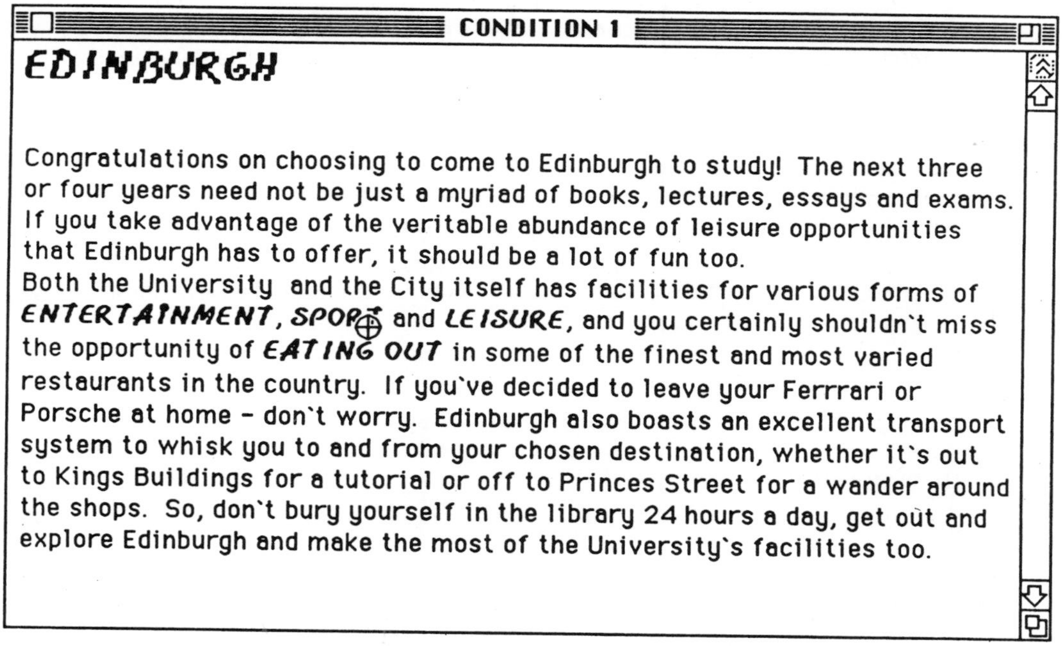

CONDITION 1

EDINBURGH

Congratulations on choosing to come to Edinburgh to study! The next three or four years need not be just a myriad of books, lectures, essays and exams. If you take advantage of the veritable abundance of leisure opportunities that Edinburgh has to offer, it should be a lot of fun too.
Both the University and the City itself has facilities for various forms of **ENTERTAINMENT**, **SPORT** and **LEISURE**, and you certainly shouldn't miss the opportunity of **EATING OUT** in some of the finest and most varied restaurants in the country. If you've decided to leave your Ferrrari or Porsche at home — don't worry. Edinburgh also boasts an excellent transport system to whisk you to and from your chosen destination, whether it's out to Kings Buildings for a tutorial or off to Princes Street for a wander around the shops. So, don't bury yourself in the library 24 hours a day, get out and explore Edinburgh and make the most of the University's facilities too.

Fig 1 *Top level of hierarchy condition.*

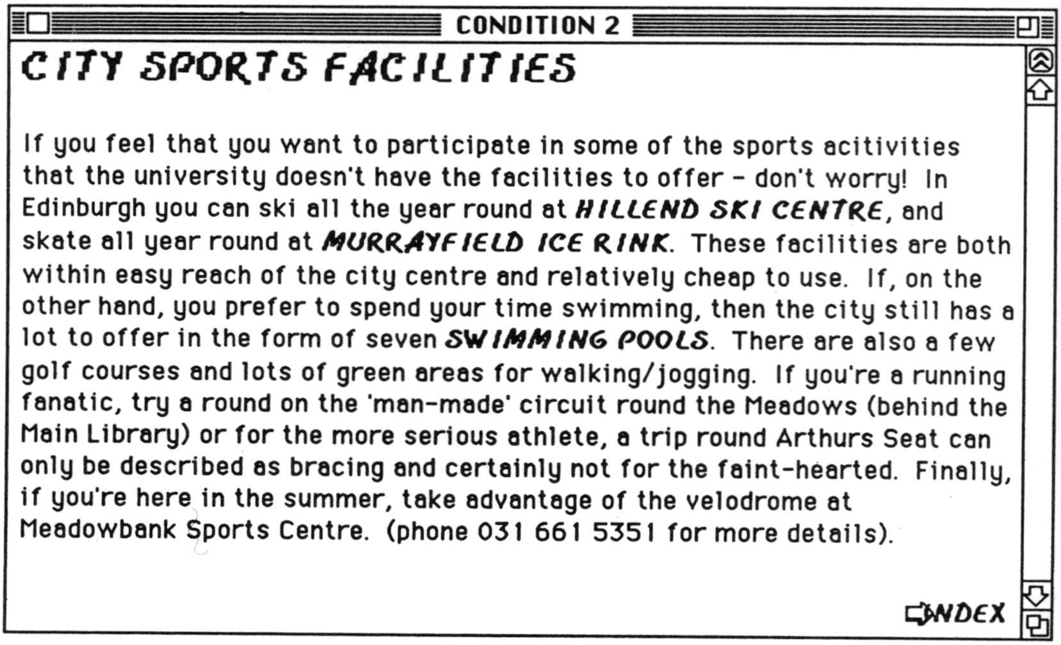

```
┌─────────────────────────────── CONDITION 2 ───────────────────────────────┐
│                                                                            │
│  CITY SPORTS FACILITIES                                                    │
│                                                                            │
│  If you feel that you want to participate in some of the sports acitivities│
│  that the university doesn't have the facilities to offer - don't worry! In│
│  Edinburgh you can ski all the year round at HILLEND SKI CENTRE, and       │
│  skate all year round at MURRAYFIELD ICE RINK. These facilities are both   │
│  within easy reach of the city centre and relatively cheap to use. If, on the│
│  other hand, you prefer to spend your time swimming, then the city still has a│
│  lot to offer in the form of seven SWIMMING POOLS. There are also a few    │
│  golf courses and lots of green areas for walking/jogging. If you're a running│
│  fanatic, try a round on the 'man-made' circuit round the Meadows (behind the│
│  Main Library) or for the more serious athlete, a trip round Arthurs Seat can│
│  only be described as bracing and certainly not for the faint-hearted. Finally,│
│  if you're here in the summer, take advantage of the velodrome at          │
│  Meadowbank Sports Centre. (phone 031 661 5351 for more details).          │
│                                                                            │
│                                                                     INDEX  │
└────────────────────────────────────────────────────────────────────────────┘
```

Fig 2 *Typical screen in mixed and index conditions.*

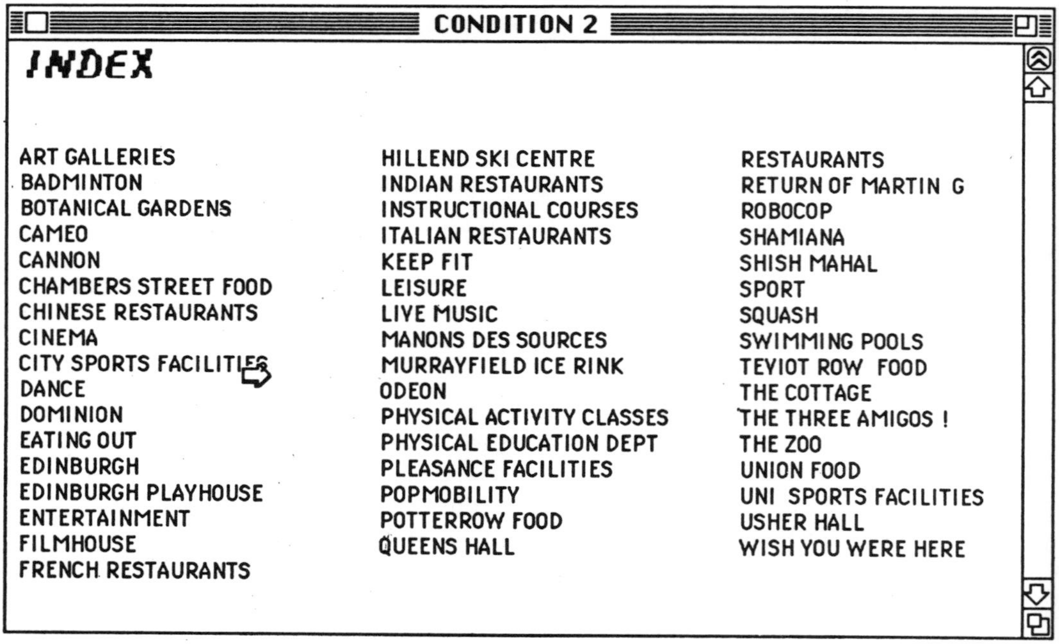

```
┌─────────────────────────────── CONDITION 2 ───────────────────────────────┐
│                                                                            │
│  INDEX                                                                     │
│                                                                            │
│  ART GALLERIES           HILLEND SKI CENTRE         RESTAURANTS            │
│  BADMINTON               INDIAN RESTAURANTS         RETURN OF MARTIN G     │
│  BOTANICAL GARDENS       INSTRUCTIONAL COURSES      ROBOCOP                │
│  CAMEO                   ITALIAN RESTAURANTS        SHAMIANA               │
│  CANNON                  KEEP FIT                   SHISH MAHAL            │
│  CHAMBERS STREET FOOD    LEISURE                    SPORT                  │
│  CHINESE RESTAURANTS     LIVE MUSIC                 SQUASH                 │
│  CINEMA                  MANONS DES SOURCES         SWIMMING POOLS         │
│  CITY SPORTS FACILITIES  MURRAYFIELD ICE RINK       TEVIOT ROW  FOOD       │
│  DANCE                   ODEON                      THE COTTAGE            │
│  DOMINION                PHYSICAL ACTIVITY CLASSES  THE THREE AMIGOS !     │
│  EATING OUT              PHYSICAL EDUCATION DEPT    THE ZOO                │
│  EDINBURGH               PLEASANCE FACILITIES       UNION FOOD             │
│  EDINBURGH PLAYHOUSE     POPMOBILITY                UNI  SPORTS FACILITIES │
│  ENTERTAINMENT           POTTERROW FOOD             USHER HALL             │
│  FILMHOUSE               QUEENS HALL                WISH YOU WERE HERE     │
│  FRENCH RESTAURANTS                                                        │
│                                                                            │
└────────────────────────────────────────────────────────────────────────────┘
```

Fig 3 *Index screen.*

Index condition

This form of the hypertext was simply the alphabetical index with no hierarchical structure at all. Thus, every screen was still immediately available from every other screen via the index, but any hierarchy that the subjects might perceive could not be directly traversed. The embedded titles of other screens were bold but not active. See Figs 2 and Fig 3.

The bold items (other than the screen's title) are links to further screens of information in the Mixed Condition, but inactive in the Index Condition.

Each item (other than the screen's title) is a link to the appropriate screen in both the Mixed and Index Conditions.

Search tasks and card sorting

In order that the subjects would have as similar a level of exposure to the hypertext document as possible, they were asked to perform a series of search tasks. Every odd numbered question was designed to be easier to answer by traversing the hierarchy, and every even numbered question by using the index. For example, a question easier to answer using the hierarchical structure would be 'Which cinema is showing the film "Roxanne"?' and one easier to answer using the index structure might be 'Who are the main actors in the film "The Three Amigos"?'. This was done both to avoid one system being much easier than any other to use and also to promote a balanced mix of search strategy in the Mixed Condition.

The time taken per task and screens searched per task were recorded to give information on the efficiency of search and the mean time taken.

In an effort to determine any cognitive representation of the hypertext that the subjects might have, they were asked to perform a card-laying task. The subjects were asked to lay cards, with reduced versions of the screen on them, on a large board exactly as they imagined them to be arranged in the document and also to draw any connecting computer links that they thought existed between these screens. This technique for determining the subject's knowledge of the data structure has previously been used by Parton *et al* (1985).

A questionnaire was developed to examine other possible variables that might be responsible for any effects found and also try to form some understanding of what was actually happening when subjects reported feeling 'lost'.

It was hypothesized that if the subjects were attempting to cognitively represent the data structure, the users of the Mixed hypertext would have the process of cognitive map development, as proposed by Siegel and White (1975), disrupted. That is, as they tried to connect various areas together to form minimaps, or tried to connect minimaps together to form full survey maps, they would have difficulties in deciding where one minimap should be placed in relation to the others. This is because the index allows them to go directly to a section completely unrelated to a part of the hierarchy that has just been examined. Disruption would also occur because there are at least two potential models of the structure, the hierarchy and the index.

The value of the information about the structure of the hypertext varies between conditions. Knowledge of the structure is most valuable in the Hierarchy Condition, since it is the only means of navigating through the hypertext. Knowledge of the structure is least valuable in the Mixed Condition, since the required screen could be found using the hierarchical links or more directly via the index. Also, the complexity of the hypertext structure varies between conditions. The Index Condition structure is the most simple (the index screen is linked to every other screen), and the Mixed Condition structure is the most complex (both hierarchical and index structures are present).

It was expected that these differences between conditions would be evident in a variety of ways. Firstly the mean task performance times for subjects in the Mixed Condition would show a much slower improvement over time, that is subjects in the Hierarchy and Index Conditions would show a faster decrease in mean task time as their conceptually simpler systems would be much quicker to become familiar with.

Also, the Mixed hypertext would be less efficiently used than the others, that is the subjects would search a larger number of screens per question, because the subjects would have the least sophisticated representation of the structure (because knowledge of the structure is the least valuable and the most complex).

Further evidence for incomplete spatial cognitive representation was expected to be seen by the Mixed subjects' models being less spatial in nature (cards layed in groups of siblings) and more procedural in nature (cards laid 'parent-child, parent-child').

More direct evidence for the formation of the spatial cognitive map would be that subjects in the Hierarchy Condition would have the greatest knowledge of structure, again determined from the card layout task, since they should have reached the most advanced stage of cognitive map development. Index Condition subjects would be expected to have good knowledge of the hypertext structure, as, despite being of little value for navigation, it has a very simple model.

The frequency of being 'lost', as reported via the questionnaire, was expected to be somewhat different for subjects in the Mixed Condition, as was the form of being 'lost'. The forms of being 'lost' that were looked at are as outlined by Elm and Woods (1985) :

- not knowing where to go next;

- knowing where to go, but not knowing how to get there;

- not knowing where they were in the overall structure of the document.

If subjects were creating spatial cognitive maps as suggested, and the Mixed subjects were experiencing difficulties with this, then it was hypothesized that they would experience being 'lost' more frequently and also that this would be most often in the form of 'not knowing where they were in the overall structure of the document'.

Method

The subject group recruited for this experiment consisted of 27 university undergraduates comprising 15 males and 12 females, with a mean age of 20.5 years and little or no computing experience. Subjects were randomly allocated one of the three structures of the hypertext document and their performance on each of the three parts of each condition, search task, card-sort and questionnaire, was compared using a between-subjects design.

The experimental apparatus consisted of an Apple Macintosh micro computer, mouse and mouse pad. The hypertext documents used were produced using the software package Guide (produced by Office Workstations Limited), then converted to read-only documents using Guide Envelope.

Links or buttons in a document could be recognized in two ways. Firstly (for the purposes of this experiment) they appeared in bold type, and secondly, the mouse cursor changed shape when moved over them. All buttons were actioned by the user clicking the mouse once.

The hypertext documents looked as similar as possible for all three conditions of the experiment, varying only in their structure and the availability of an index, as described earlier.

The subjects' interactions with the documents were recorded with a video camera to produce a time-stamped video tape of the computer screen and the subject's voice for later analysis.

Fifty 9 cm x 5.5 cm cards of the screens in the hypertext were printed with the titles enlarged (for legibility) and were layed out on a 6' x 4' white board. Connections between the cards were drawn with a whiteboard dry-marker pen.

In the first part of the experiment subjects were shown the experimental hypertext document after spending a small amount of time on a training document to familiarize themselves with moving around a hypertext. They were told they would be asked 20 questions, the answers to which could be found somewhere in the text of the document and they were asked to give their answers verbally. It was stressed that there were no trick questions, that the answers would always be explicitly expressed, and that even if the subjects happened to know the answer to a particular question, they should still attempt to find the screen with the appropriate information on it.

It was stressed that this was not a speed test, but that subjects should try to work through the tasks at a steady rate. The option of moving on to the next question was available if subjects felt that they could not find the answer to a particular question. Each question in turn was asked verbally and a slip of paper with the question printed on it was placed nearby for reference.

This section of the experiment was video recorded and a score was taken of the number of questions that the subject successfully managed to answer.

Secondly, subjects were taken to another part of the room and shown the white board with the cards arranged in random order on the right hand side. They were informed that these were all the screens of information that were available to them in the hypertext document and that their task was to lay them out as they imagined them to be arranged in the hypertext document.

The whole screen, and not just the title, was used for each card as some subjects may have been remembering the actual shape of the text or the screen layout. It was stressed that subjects should not read the small text on the cards, only the titles. This was to avoid this part of the experiment becoming simply a deductive construction task. Before they attempted this task, the subjects were informed that after they had laid the cards out they would be asked to draw any connections that they thought existed between the cards. A score was then recorded of the amount of cards correctly placed. This was calculated by one mark being awarded for every card directly connected to its parent card. The way subjects laid out the cards was also categorized as being predominantly procedural, spatial or neither.

Finally, subjects were given the questionnaire to complete, and a copy of the question list to refer to.

Results and discussion

Video data

The number of questions correctly answered varied very little between the three conditions, with most subjects scoring over 80% correct.

The mean time per task was calculated for each subject, from which the mean task time per question for each condition was computed. See Table 1.

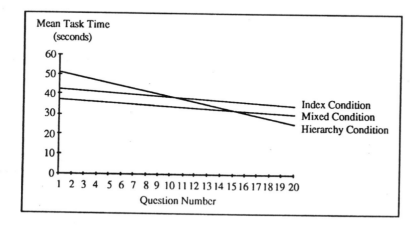

Table 1 *Regression graph of mean task time*

As can be seen from the graph in Table 1, there was a noticeable gradual decrease in the time per task for the Hierarchy Condition, while the time per task in the Mixed and Index Conditions remained relatively constant. (Note that the values of the mean task time cannot be compared since the minimum number of screens that needed to be searched per question in each condition were different.)

The mean number of screens searched per question were calculated for each subject, then combined to produce a mean for each of the three conditions. These were then compared with the minimum number of screens per question for each condition to produce a measure of efficiency of system use. A Kruskal-Wallis test on these measures revealed that the hypertext used most efficiently was the Index hypertext and the hypertext used the least efficiently was the Mixed hypertext (H = 4.835, df = 2, P < 0.1).

Subjects in the Mixed Condition showed a slower decrease in mean task time than subjects in the Hierarchy Condition, suggesting that the Mixed hypertext was more difficult to 'get to know', although this also applies to the Index Condition. The Mixed hypertext was also found to be the least efficiently used. Taken together, these results suggest that there is something about the form of the Mixed hypertext that makes it inherently more difficult to use than the others. Perhaps this difficulty is a result of the continual disruption of attempts by subjects at forming survey-type cognitive maps of the hypertext.

Card layout data

Hierarchy condition

All of the layouts in the Hierarchy Condition had a hierarchical form but varied in the directions in which they were layed. For example, most subjects placed the top level card 'EDINBURGH' at the top of the working area and had the tree progressing vertically down from it. Others were laid from left to right, with the top level at the left hand side. One subject laid the hierarchy in a 'sunburst' form with the top level card in the centre of the board and the branches of the tree radiating outward from it.

Mixed condition

Most of the layouts by subjects in the Mixed Condition had a hierarchical form, although this varied between small sections, or 'minimaps', of hierarchy with the top card only connected to the index card and complete, largely accurate, hierarchies with subjects also realizing the position of the index card in the structure (i.e. connected to every card). However, there was one subject who laid out a hierarchy but thought that the index was not connected to anything at all. Several layouts produced were in the form of an index. These were mainly laid in three alphabetically arranged columns, but subjects also demonstrated knowledge of some of the hierarchical connections between the cards by drawing those in too.

Index condition

The Index Condition produced as varied a range of layouts as the Mixed Condition. Several subjects layed out very accurate hierarchies and were also aware of the fact that the only connections that actually existed were the ones between the index and every card. When questioned about this they informed the experimenter that they imagined the information to be arranged in a hierarchical form and considered using the index as merely a method of traversing this perceived hierarchy. One subject produced a layout that was a mixture of index and hierarchy, and another subject produced no layout at all, claiming that he had no idea at all of how the information was arranged. Perhaps a cognitive map was of so little value for this form of the hypertext that none was formed.

Discussion

The layout forms on the whole conformed to expectations, which appears to support the hypothesis of the cognitive representation being at a more advanced 'spatial', survey-type stage for the systems with the simplest structures.

In the layout procedure, none of the layouts were purely procedural in nature. Most of the spatial layouts were produced in the Index Condition, and least spatial layouts were produced in the Mixed Condition. Most of the layouts in all conditions showed both spatial and procedural elements.

The spatial card laying usually occurred at the top of any hierarchy or piece of hierarchy that was laid, while the procedural laying tended to occur towards the bottom or leaf areas of hierarchy, or in areas that had either not been visited often or not been visited at all during the tasks. Thus it would appear that subjects are attempting to 'place' each screen of information in relation to the other screens as they are encountered in some sort of cognitive representation, this representation for each card becoming more accurate and fixed with each encounter. This may support the developmental sequence proposed by Siegel & White (1975) for physical environments, with the representation progressing from landmark recognition to procedural or route map form, then through minimap form, and finally to full survey map form. In which case it would then support the hypothesis that the difficulty for subjects in the Mixed Condition was the continual disruption of the development of a cognitive representation. Alternatively the subjects may never get beyond the minimap form of representation, although subjects in the Hierarchy and Index Conditions appeared to have more developed cognitive models of the hypertext structure, which lends weight to the development hypothesis.

Further support was lent to the cognitive representation hypothesis by some of the layouts in the Index Condition. Several of the subjects in this condition arranged the cards in the form of a hierarchy despite the fact that they could not directly traverse the hierarchy during the tasks (the hierarchy was visible in this condition by the screen title buttons being in bold, but not active). The subjects commented that they were aware that screens were only accessible from the index, but that they imagined the data as having a hierarchical structure and simply used the index as a navigation tool to traverse this perceived hierarchy. Thus it was not necessary for subjects to directly traverse the hierarchy to perceive of hierarchical connections between the screens, suggesting perhaps that subjects were attempting to organize the data in some way.

The scores that each subject was given for their layout in the card-sort task were compared using a Kruskal-Wallis test which showed significant differences in subjects' knowledge of structure between the three conditions. This knowledge was greatest for Hierarchy, then for Index, and least for Mixed ($H = 8.66$, $df = 2$, $p < 0.02$). This knowledge of the structure supports the hypothesis that subjects in the Hierarchy and Index Conditions would have the greatest knowledge and those in Mixed the least. It suggests again that there is difficulty in acquiring a conceptual model of the structure of the hypertext document in Mixed.

Questionnaire data

The subjects' responses to questions in the questionnaire were analysed using Kruskal-Wallis tests to determine if there were significant differences between conditions in the ratings given to:

- satisfaction of interaction;

- clarity of information within the document;

- understanding of how to use the computer;

- difficulty of the tasks.

'Satisfaction of interaction' was found to be significantly different between the conditions, with the subjects in the Hierarchy Condition reporting most satisfaction. The Mixed Condition received the second lowest rating, with its mean rating being marginally above that of Index, which was reported to be the least satisfying to use ($H = 5.78$, $df = 2$, $p < 0.1$). There were no significant differences found between the conditions for ratings given to the other three items.

This highest 'Satisfaction of Interaction' rating for the Hierarchy Condition was possibly because the data conformed to a structure that was relatively easy to conceptualize in terms of chunks or minimaps. The middle satisfaction rating was given to the Mixed Condition. If cognitive representation is occurring then the Mixed hypertext is probably not very satisfying to use because it is difficult to connect any areas of data together to produce a view of the overall structure of the document. Quite surprisingly, the Index hypertext received the lowest satisfaction rating, although this was only fractionally lower than the rating given to Mixed. This was possibly because the apparent attempts at organization seen in the card layouts produced by subjects in the Index Condition were much more difficult as the hierarchy could be seen but not directly traversed, thereby causing the system to be somewhat frustrating to use.

Subjects were also asked which questions they found to be especially difficult. The proportion of subjects in each condition that reported at least one such question were Hierarchy 50%, Mixed 80%, Index 60%. The reasons given for questions being difficult were usually along the lines of the information not being where the subjects expected it to be, or the subject not being able to decide where to search for the information.

In answers to other questions, several subjects in each condition reported feeling 'lost' while doing the tasks. The proportions of subjects in each condition reporting this were Hierarchy 30%, Mixed 70%, Index 50%. While this shows that more of the subjects in the Mixed Condition owned to feeling 'lost', this result was not significant (Chi-Square test with $c2 = 3.2$, $df = 2$).

The particular form of feeling lost reported by subjects also varied between the conditions and had the profile shown in Table 2.

Form of being 'lost'	Hierarchy Condition	Mixed Condition	Index Condition
Not knowing where to go next.	2	7	3
Knowing where to go, but not knowing how to get there.	-	3	-
Not knowing where they were in relation to the overall structure of the document.	1	4	1

Table 2 *Form of being 'lost' reported*

As can be seen from Table 2, in the Mixed Condition more subjects reported each form of feeling lost than subjects in any of the other conditions. Additionally, these subjects were the only ones to express feeling the form of being lost where they 'knew where to go but didn't know how to get there'. Finally, they also reported a feeling of 'not knowing where they were in relation to the overall structure of the document' than subjects in either of the other two conditions.

The particular questions found to be especially difficult for subjects in each condition also lend support to the cognitive mapping hypothesis. Question 4, 'Where are the dance classes held?' was frequently found to be reported as difficult by subjects in the Hierarchy Condition. This could have been for two reasons. Firstly, the question involved the first search of the deepest branch of the hierarchy and thus subjects were encountering a great deal of new 'territory' which would perhaps have to be incorporated into the current conceptual model. Secondly, the screen to be found, *Dance*, was actually within the category of *Sport*, but could equally have been in *Entertainment* or *Leisure*. Thus the general area in which the answer could be found was not obvious and possibly did not conform to the expectations of the subjects. This emphasizes the problems of categorizing hierarchical structures and also illustrates the influence that hierarchical categories have on users' conceptual models and their expectations of the probable contents of those categories.

The question most difficult for Index subjects was number 17, 'What is a Kakori Kebab made from ?'. This was probably found to be easier by subjects in the Hierarchy Condition as they had the support of the hierarchy. That is, knowing that a kebab is an item of food, they could search within the area of *Eating out*. However, subjects in the Index Condition could only look at index items that might be related to food without knowing the contents and boundaries of the appropriate section, or try to find this information by laboriously traversing the perceived hierarchy via the index.

More subjects in the Mixed Condition found at least one of the tasks especially difficult, although no particular question stood out as being especially difficult. Given that the subjects had both search methods available, this could have been the result of difficulties in choosing which strategy to use, or general distress at being unable to form a cognitive map of the structure causing a degradation in user performance.

Correlational measures

The following correlational measures were computed from the data using the Spearman Rank Correlation Coefficient.

Knowledge of structure was positively correlated with the reporting of feeling lost, i.e. those with least knowledge of the overall structure of the document were also those who most often expressed feeling lost. The result was a positive correlation between the two measures, with $r = 0.488$, which was significant at the $P < 0.01$ level for a one-tailed test.

Knowledge of structure was also positively correlated with the satisfaction rating given to the system used ($r = 0.33$, $P < 0.05$ for a one-tailed test). Thus it appears that some of the satisfaction expressed by users is related to the amount they knew about how the information was arranged.

The correlation between satisfaction rating and being lost (in all forms) also suggests that knowledge of the arrangement of the information and of the user's current position within it was an important factor for the individuals using this system ($r = 0.467$, $P < 0.01$ for a one-tailed test). Therefore, the subjects giving their interaction with the document the lowest ratings also most often reported being 'lost'.

Conclusions

The subject population was atypical in that it consisted of university undergraduates in their early twenties. This would present difficulties when trying to extend the results to make predictions about the behaviour of the general population.

Refinements of this study could be made to the classification of the form of the layout in the card-layout task. The layouts were classified by the experimenter who was aware of which hypertext structure the subject had been exposed to.

The database used for this experiment consisted of items that were 'naturally' hierarchically organized. That is, most individuals would classify the data in this way themselves, eg. *Odeon, Cannon* and *Dominion* under the heading of *Cinema*. This was done to make the experiment as naturalistic as possible, as information systems encountered by the general public would probably have this type of 'natural' hierarchy. A further experiment could be designed to look at what would happen when using a database of, for example, nonsense syllables.

The subjects in this study who used the Mixed hypertext frequently used the index available in the following way. Firstly they would access a general area of the document, eg. cinema, which they would then explore using the hierarchy. The index was only used to access a specific screen directly if the user had difficulties in finding it using the other method, or had reached a later stage in the tasks, suggesting that they were more familiar with the document.

Our conclusion is that individuals appear to be attempting to create cognitive representations of hypertext structures in the form of a survey-type map, and the difficulties of doing so for users of a mixed-structure hypertext has implications for the way hypertext documents are structured and for the types of orientating or navigation devices available to hypertext readers.

Readers should be allowed to develop a cognitive map of one view of the data structure before being given the option of navigating through the data some other way. This could be implemented in two ways. Firstly, readers could be advised only to use one search method until they felt quite familiar with the data structure. Secondly, the document could have two types of index available, where one is a contents screen (similar to that normally found in text books), and another reflects more directly the 'minimap' representation readers are likely to develop, i.e. an index of main sections linked to their own more detailed contents.

The most appropriate types of navigation devices would be those that are spatially-based, i.e. present the information structure in a 2- or 3-dimensional form, rather than those which simply keep account of the names of the screens viewed by the user, although Conklin (1987) has demonstrated the difficulties that occur using a 2-dimensional representation when the number of links between data items become extensive.

A spatially-based navigation device has been used very effectively by Tom Hewett (1987) in The Drexel Disk. This is a form of electronic 'guidebook' which runs on the Macintosh personal computer and is given to freshmen entering Drexel University in Philadelphia. The Drexel Disk uses graphics to present spatial information and also provides recall cues to help locate and retrieve information. Given the findings of this study and the fact that the Drexel students reported that they liked the overall organization of their Disk, perhaps we should look towards methods normally used for making physical environments more memorable and navigable and apply these to help prevent users becoming 'lost in hyperspace'.

References

Canter D, Rivers R and Storrs G (1985) Characterizing user navigation through complex data structures. *Behaviour and Information Technology* 4 (2): 93-102.

Charney D (1987) Comprehending non-linear text: the role of discourse cues and reading strategies. *Proceedings of HyperTEXT '87*, Chapel Hill, North Carolina, November 13-15. pp 109-120.

Cohen R and Schuepfer T (1980) The representation of landmarks and routes. *Child Development* 51. pp 1065-1071.

Conklin J (1987) Hypertext: an introduction and survey. *IEEE Computer* 20 (9): 17-41.

Elm W C and Woods D D (1985) Getting lost: a case study in interface design. *Proceedings of the Human Factors Society*. pp 927-931.

Gilfoil D M (1982) Warming up to computers: a study of cognitive and affective interaction over time. *Proceedings of the Gaithersburg Human Factors in Computer Systems Conference*, March 15-17, Gaithersburg, Maryland. pp 245-250.

Hewett T (1987) The drexel disk: an electronic 'guidebook'. In: *People and Computers III*. Edited by Diaper D and Winder R. Cambridge University Press, Cambridge. pp 115-129.

Jones W P (1987) How do we distinguish the hyper from the hype in non-linear text? In: *Human-Computer Interaction - INTERACT'87*. Edited by Bullinger H J and Schackel B. Elsevier Science Publishers BV, North-Holland.

Mahony K (1988) Navigation round hypertext. Working Paper K7, Alvey Fortune Project. Computing Laboratory, University of Kent, Canterbury.

Parton D, Huffman K, Pridgen P, Norman K and Shneiderman B (1985) Learning a menu selection tree: training methods compared. *Behaviour and Information Technology* 4 (2): 81-91.

Siegel R and White T (1975) The development of spatial representations of large-scale environments. In: *Advances in Child Development and Behaviour*, 10. Edited by Reese H W. Academic Press, New York.

8

S J Harland[1]

Human factors engineering and interface development: a hypertext tool aiding prototyping activity

Abstract

A description and evaluation of the use of hypertext in a prototyping activity for display design. Guide is described as being used in three modes of activity: task analytic, system development and human factors engineering.

Introduction

The research at the Behavioural Science Division of the Admiralty Research Establishment which exploits a hypertext tool forms part of a programme investigating the derivation of optimal design solutions within a prototyping environment. The specific concern of that programme is information management and dialogue structure and, therefore, the research aims to understand the set of design principles that lead to the derivation of effective structures. The hypertext application Guide™ is being used, firstly as a (limited) simulation tool for the purpose of machinery control task analysis and secondly, as a prototyping tool for the purpose of machinery control interface development.

In this chapter I will attempt to locate the Behavioural Science Division (BSD) research which exploits hypertext within the context of a prototyping activity for optimal display design, within which a number of levels of research will be identified. In order to do this I will use a framework from Long (1986) which characterizes HCI activities, in order to make explicit the various contributions of science and engineering to system development in general and interface development in particular within a prototyping environment. This framework is important because the contribution that hypertext tools can make to the process of prototyping can be made explicit and therefore assessed according to some criterion.

Because the hypertext meeting out of which this chapter has arisen was conducted under the auspices of the Alvey HCI Club SIG on Interactive Learning Systems (ILS), I should make clear that the learning process referred to primarily involves the researcher.

System development paradigm

The framework from Long (1986) characterizes different HCI activities in terms of science, engineering and system development paradigms.[2] The real world is contrasted with the representational world whose function is to facilitate understanding or change of the real world. The science paradigm aims at establishing truths concerning the world and possesses the type of knowledge relating to phenomena whose measurement (methods) and explanation (theories) are required to be made explicit. The engineering paradigm concerns the knowledge and practice involved in the application of scientific knowledge in the development of artifacts (ie their performance and principles of operation). Here the criterion is not whether a proposition is true, but whether an artifact works.

However, science and engineering knowledge alone do not produce systems for use in the real world. To achieve this aim requires the activities of the system development paradigm whose aim is the fulfilment of individual and/or social need in the real world. See Fig 1.

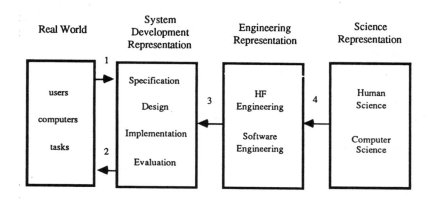

Fig 1 *Model of activities associated with the System Development paradigm. Arrows are transformations defined as follows: 1 . analyse, 2. synthesize, 3. apply, 4. particularize.*

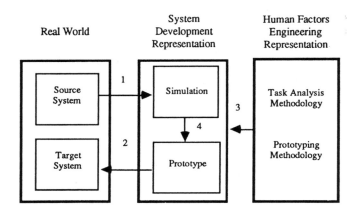

Fig 2 *Model of simulation and prototyping activities within the System Development paradigm. Transformations as follows: 1. analyse, 2. synthesize, 3. apply, 4. derive.*

In the model, engineering knowledge is applied by two transformations, apply and synthesize. Application produces a system development representation comprising a specification representation (of system purpose, intended users and physical and social environment), a design representation (explicit, coherent and complete form of the specification for the purpose of programming), an implementation representation (program), and the evaluation representation (used to compare and assess the system against the specification).

Prototype Research

Using the framework in Fig 1, the model in Fig 2 attempts to make explicit the contribution of a prototyping methodology which would enable prototype solutions to be derived from a source system (via a simulation) for the purposes of influencing a target system (Campion and Long, 1987)[3]. Note that the HFE Representation involves the utilization of science knowledge in the development of artifacts, although this is not shown in the figure.

   The Human Factors engineer derives knowledge from the real world (source system) by using an appropriate analytic technique (methodology), the source system description taking the form of some task model generated for a purpose (eg to support a simulation). From the simulation, features of the system can be modified (prototyped) in order to explore the potential benefits accrued from new configurations associated with the system entities (user, computer, and/or their interaction). It is, however, important to note that the facility on which the system is prototyped must have sufficient flexibility (with respect to the hardware and/or software) to allow proper manipulation and assessment of the system entities under investigation.

If the prototyping activity is successful (ie, the product satisfies some predefined performance criterion), the associated system development representation (eg one that could instantiate the specification in terms of a program) can then be carried forward for the purpose of influencing the target system. By prototyping I mean an activity which must involve the manipulation of some attribute associated with a system entity (user, computer, and/or their interaction), appropriate to a system development stage (eg specification, design, implementation) for the purpose of influencing a target system towards optimal design (against some agreed criterion)[4].

We can therefore define the BSD prototyping research as requirements prototyping which involves the manipulation of interface dialogue structures for the purpose of influencing next generation machinery control systems towards optimal support of user interaction tasks.

This research is supported by three modes of activity:

1. the Task Analytic mode involves the derivation of machinery control task models which can be applied to support system development;

2. the System Development mode involves the derivation of a machinery control dialogue structure via prototyping, by which process the researcher can learn more about the requirements for a design methodology;

3. the HF Engineering mode involves the derivation of a design methodology to aid interface prototyping.

Guide

Use of Guide™ is made within the second mode of activity as a tool to aid interface prototyping activity on a micro computer (Macintosh Plus™) and within the third mode during analysis as a simulation tool.

Mapping the BSD research activities onto the model of HF Engineering and System Development (Figure 2), Guide™ is at present being used as a simulation tool for the purposes of simulating a menu structure from a source system, in this case the Canadian Shipboard Integrated Machinery Control System (SHINMACS) (Gorrell, 1982). From this simulation the researcher can learn more about the machinery control tasks and, in conjunction with other information, the optimization of displays for the support of the user tasks.

The second (intended) use of Guide™ is as a prototyping tool for the purposes of interface development, the selection of an optimal design depending on the criterion of effectiveness adopted (eg fulfilling some operational requirement). In addition, this second stage, during subsequent prototyping exercises, could serve the purpose of validating any methodology developed during earlier exercises.

The nature of the simulation involved in the initial use of Guide™ is determined by a functionality at the user interface (ie display page relations and their representation) and at the application interface (ie, real world object attribute relations and their representation). See Fig 3.

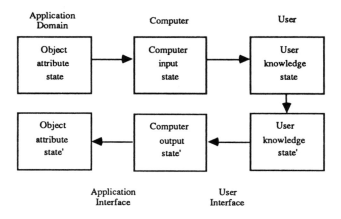

Fig 3 *Model of application domain, computer and user states and the transformations between these states through application and user interfaces.*

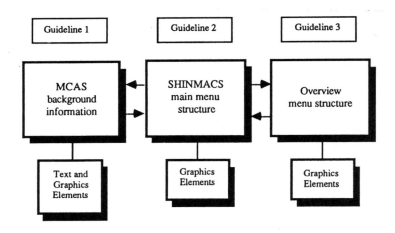

Fig 4a *Structure within which relations between Guideline documents are established and the composition of those documents.*

The functionality at the user interface (that which is to be prototyped) is realized by a network of hypertext links established within and between the hypertext documents[5] . The functionality at the application interface would be determined by inputs from a computer model representing the attribute states of the domain objects (eg a computer model of some plant and its behaviour). However, these inputs are not represented within the current system and, therefore, the degree of functionality associated with this aspect of the simulation is severely limited.

With respect to the user interface functionality, Fig 4a shows the framework within which the relations between Guideline documents are structured. The SHINMACS menu structure comprises the central document (which consists of graphic elements) with connections to two other documents; the first contains machinery control and surveillance (MCAS) background information which consists of text and graphic elements; and the second an overview menu structure which consists of graphic elements.

The motivation for separating the overview menu from the main SHINMACS menu stems from the requirement to have both menus displayed simultaneously, although only one menu structure (window) will be active at any point in time.

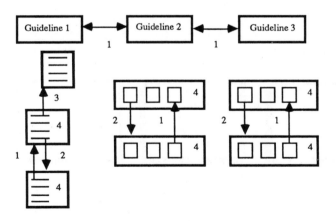

Fig 4b *Detailed representation of the inter- and intra-document links (arrows) using Guide. The links are defined as follows; 1. reference link; 2. replacement link; 3. note link. 4 signifies an inquiry set (see text).*

Fig 4b presents a more detailed view of the Guide™ links within and between documents. The various links are opened by the activation of buttons specified within a document:

1. activation of a reference button moves the user to a new part of the document with automatic backtracking function;

2. activation of a replacement button replaces the button with a segment of text and/or graphics;

3. activation of the note button opens a hidden footnote.

An inquiry function is provided to enable more complex structuring of connections within a document. Used in conjunction with a set of replacement buttons an inquiry enables a mutually exclusive selection to be made. This particular combination is extensively used in the menu selection procedure.[6]

It is important to note that Guide™ is initially being used in a way that constrains how the user interacts with the computer to execute a task by presenting a fixed menu structure. Ultimately, during the stage of interface prototyping, these constraints will be relaxed to provide the flexibility necessary to explore new dialogue structures which give optimum support to user tasks by way of supporting User Interaction Models (UIM) (Long, 1987). A UIM is a mental representation of a system entity (eg computer) created by a user for the purpose of understanding and predicting the system entity behaviour.[7]

Designer's conceptual model

Ideally, when a system is constructed the design will be based around a Designer's Conceptual Model (DCM) of the system which will govern the design of the user interface for the purpose of user acquisition, ie, the representation seen by the user should be consistent, coherent and intelligible (Norman, 1983). But this intelligibility at the interface will rely on a correspondence between the UIM and the DCM, if that UIM is to be useful for the purposes of interaction with the computer.

Hypertext tools can make a contribution at the implementation of the DCM where there is a requirement for more than one level of description of the entity attributes necessary to support the user task at the interface. Indeed, there are generally three relevant levels of system description to a control task (Rasmussen, 1984) which could provide a framework for establishing hypertext mappings between levels. See Fig 5.

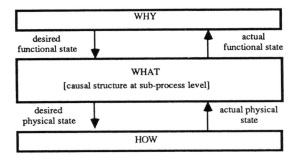

Fig 5 *Levels of system description relevant to a control task. Desired states are defined by higer (more functional) levels of description and this requirement is represented by downward arrows. Actual states are defined by lower (more physical) levels of description and this constraint is represented by upward arrows.*

Why level: the intention behind the (sub) process. Any planning for recovery from an identified disturbance must represent an acceptable compromise between the capabilities of the physical plant (in a disturbed state) and the design intention as reflected in functional requirements and constraints.

What level: the (sub) process under consideration in terms of its causal structure and operational state described independently of implementation detail.

How level: the implementation of the (sub) process. Configuration monitoring and control are dependent on a given plant and require search and localization activity within an equipment-based structure.

The level selected by the user would be appropriate for the decision-making required at that particular point in time and would require a flexibility in system representation at the interface.

Conclusion

What hypertext offers, therefore, is the potential for an author (researcher/ designer) to establish a network of interconnected nodes of information for the purpose of supporting users' exploration of a problem space which is circumscribed by the scope of that information. A network is conceived to be a set of relations which constrains users' navigation through the display domain and a node is conceived to be a collection of information gathered for a purpose and incorporating the options for navigation to other nodes.

References

Campion T J and Long J (1987) Assessing colour assignments to tactical plan displays of naval command systems. A methodology and demonstration. *Ergonomics Unit Report*, University College, London.

Gorrell E M (1981) Human Engineering Design Requirements for SHINMACS Machinery Control Consoles, Part III. Console Displays and Operation. *DCIEM Report* Number 81-R-18.

Johnson-Laird P N (1983) *Mental Models*. Cambridge University Press, Cambridge.

Long J (1986) People and computers: designing for usability. An introduction to HCI-86. In: *People and Computers*. Edited by Harrison M and Monk A. Cambridge University Press, Cambridge.

Long J (1987) A framework for user models. In: *Contemporary Ergonomics*, Proceedings of the Ergonomics Annual Conference. Edited by Magaw E D. Taylor and Francis, London.

Norman D A (1983) Some observations on mental models. In: *Mental Models*. Edited by Gentner D and Stevens A L. Lawrence Erlbaum Associates, New Jersey.

O'Bannon M (1987) Putting it in context. *MacUser*, April 1987. pp 94.98

Rasmussen J (1984) Strategies of state identification and diagnosis in supervisory control tasks and design of computer- based support systems. In: *Advances in Man-Machine Research*, Volume 1. Edited by Rouse W B. JAI Press Inc, London.

Wesley M D (1988) A guide to Guide. *MacUser*, January1988. pp 126-132.

Notes

[1]   The research described in this paper was conducted while the author was a psychologist researching into the requirements of future commanf and control systems at the Behavioural Science Division, Admiralty Research Establishment, Teddington. The author is at present a management consultant at Ronson Rhodes, London.

[2]   The term 'paradigm' denotes the activities of groups of agents and is defined by the set of shared concepts, techniques and methods for the resolution of agreed problems.

[3]   A source system is one from which knowledge is acquired, in the form of some task model, and a target system is one to which knowledge is applied (Campion and Long, 1987).

[4]   I will use this third defining feature in its weakest sense; the system to be

influenced may only be loosely defined in terms of operational requirement.

[5] More correctly, I should use the term hierarchy in relation to the structure of links as they presently stand.

[6] For a review of Guide as a Hypertext application see O'Bannon (1987) and Wesley (1988).

[7] More generally, a model is a representation which possesses a systematic relation (correspondance) to an entity, but incorporating a reduced set of attributes relative to that entity. Indeed, this systematic relation and reduction is a defining characteristic of a model (Johnson-Laird, 1983).

9

Cliff McKnight
John Richardson
Andrew Dillon

The authoring of hypertext documents

Abstract

Although it is assumed that hypertext systems allow the reader to add links to a document, several developments (eg the need for document integrity, the distribution of free programs which allow read-only access to documents) suggest that this assumption might not have widespread validity. Hence, the onus will be on the document's author to provide links sufficient to support the reader's task. As a means of assisting authors we propose and discuss the establishing of a document taxonomy and describe some experiences gained in the authoring of hypertext documents.[1]

Introduction

The recent explosion in the number of hypertext papers has fortunately not been accompanied by arguments about the nature of hypertext itself; all are agreed that the important aspects are the links between information nodes. Even if the agreement is hidden in phrases like 'the Xanalogical structure of the docuverse' (Nelson, 1988), it is there nevertheless.

Similarly, practically all writers point to the advantages (eg exploration) and disadvantages (eg navigation) of hypertext documents for the reader. However, in the present chapter, we would like to highlight some of the problems for a section of the population who we feel have been under-represented, the authors of hypertext documents.

We offer these comments on the basis of our experiences in attempting to write hypertext documents and our observations of market developments. We will briefly discuss the view that authors have been under-represented in the literature, describe the market developments referred to and finally present a brief account of our own experiences and impressions.

The ignored author

Such is the general euphoric tone of much writing about hypertext that the task of the document author gets trivialized with such phrases as 'a hypertext system allows authors to link ideas together'. Hypertext systems certainly facilitate the linking of ideas, but to focus on the ease of performing the action is to obscure the importance of the decision-making leading to the action.

It is not difficult to suggest reasons why the author has been neglected. The most obvious difference between paper and electronic documents is the one which immediately faces the reader. Hence the tendency has been to discuss problems faced by the reader. Thus we find writers like Conklin (1987) listing the major disadvantages of hypertext as 'disorientation' and 'cognitive overhead'. While the latter is discussed briefly from the author's point of view, the main discussion of both relates to the reader and Conklin concludes that system design and 'research on information filtering techniques' may at least partially resolve the problems.

Similarly, other writers are content to 'throw away' the author's task by describing hypertext systems as 'the next generation of word processing' (Marchionini and Shneiderman, 1988) while presenting cogent reader-based research strategies.

One group which has been concerned with authoring is the Concordia project at Symbolics (Walker, 1988). Concordia is a development environment for technical writers. However, the primary task of the authors involved is to publish documentation relevant to the Symbolics Lisp machine. Hence reports of the project tend to concentrate more on aspects of publishing and maintaining complex documentation. When the structuring of the documentation is discussed, the emphasis is usually on the facilities within the environment available for structuring rather than the decisions needing to be taken by the author.

In many hypertext systems being used 'for real', the distinction between author and reader is often blurred. This is particularly true in situations where a hypertext system is being used to support group authoring and use of a document (as in the Symbolics case), where the 'reader' will add links to the document, customize and annotate it, thus making the distinction between the reader and author less clear. A quote from an influential and often-cited paper entitled 'Reading and writing the electronic book' by Yankelovich *et al* (1985) serves to illustrate a general attitude:

> *'Ideally, authors and readers should have the same set of integrated tools that allow them to browse through other material during the document preparation process and to add annotations and original links as they progress through an information web. In effect, the boundary between author and reader should largely disappear'.*

However, the market developments referred to earlier appear likely to affect the more public (ie not in-house) situation. We therefore turn now to these developments.

Market developments

The sudden availability of several hypertext packages for personal computers is something which even the casual observer cannot have missed: HyperTIES (based on the earlier TIES -Morariu and Shneiderman, 1986), Guide (Brown, 1986) and Black Magic for the IBM PC and Guide and HyperCard for the Apple Macintosh. Such packages have been responsible for bringing the notion of hypertext to a wider audience than the academics who have been discussing the ideas for some 40 years (Bush, 1945; Engelbart, 1963; Nelson, 1967).

Such packages place hypertext authoring tools in the hands of many and therefore potentially increase awareness of authoring problems. However, we feel that a specific development aimed at readers has less obvious, and perhaps more serious, implications for authors. This development is the releasing into the public domain of programs allowing hypertext documents to be read.

The Guidance desk accessory version of Guide and the Black Magic Reader program are both made freely available so that readers can access documents prepared using the parent authoring system. The commercial advantages of this strategy are clear - more authors will be encouraged to distribute documents prepared in these systems if they believe that many people will be able to read them at no extra cost. While this will undoubtedly encourage the distribution of information in the form of hypertext documents (and the information files in Guide format provided with PageMaker 2 are a good example), it will mean that the authoring tools, in particular the ability to add links, will not be widely available.

Parenthetically we can consider HyperCard to be free since it is distributed with new machines and upgrades and its cost to existing users is trivial. However, for present purposes we will adopt the cynical view that Apple give it away in order to stimulate sales of memory upgrades and hard disks!

The important feature of these 'free readers' is that they limit the user to reading; documents accessed via them are effectively 'read-only', a state which HyperCard stacks can also be made into. While this has advantages in terms of document integrity, it also has important implications for the document author.

A further market development is the rise in popularity of CD-ROM as a publishing medium. Not only does this reinforce the read-only trend (although it is possible to relate annotation files to items on the CD-ROM), it also suggests that electronic documents published in this medium will tend to be large - a point to which we will return below. Indeed, working in conjunction with Office Workstations Ltd, our Project Quartet collaborators at Hatfield Polytechnic have produced an experimental CD-ROM containing a large database of information in Guide format (Archer et al, 1987).

Implications

Authors of traditional paper documents typically have to make few decisions about the high-level structure of the text. A journal article is written in clearly defined sections - abstract, methodology, references and so forth. Books are usually organized in chapters.

Once we have it in our hands, the whole of a book is accessible to us as readers. However, in front of an electronic read-only hypertext document we are at the mercy of the author since we will only be able to activate the links which the author has provided.

In this sense, the success or failure of our interaction with the document will be determined by the decisions made by the author about which nodes to link together. It's one thing to struggle with a tortuous prose style in the knowledge that at least all the information is available; it's a different matter if a linking style forces us around a path we would rather not follow. As many writers have pointed out, hypertext is, like ideas, non-linear. The problem is that not all people use the same thought 'paths'. Hence far from being a 'release from paper', the badly authored hypertext document may be more restrictive than its paper equivalent.

One approach might be to avoid the problem by linking each node to every other node. However, representing the structure generated by this 'solution' would be a horrendous task, yielding little more than visual spaghetti. More importantly, such a structure would not be representative of any underlying semantic structure. Alternatively, the StrathTutor system described in Chapter 12 by Kibby and Mayes might be thought to offer an 'automatic' approach to linking. However, the decisions involved in linking are merely replaced by the necessity to rate each card of the document on 60 dimensions. As Kibby and Mayes point out, the approach becomes less tenable as the size of the document increases.

The skills we have developed in writing for paper media need to be replaced by equivalent skills relevant to electronic media. The author whose aim is to communicate ideas must learn how best to express those ideas in the new medium. The expression of the ideas is no longer limited to the words used to encapsulate them in various nodes, but must now also be taken to include the connections between the nodes.

In order to determine the optimum links, the author needs to anticipate the uses to which the reader will put the text. In certain cases, where the user's purpose in accessing the information (that is, the user's task) is clearly defined, the author will be able to foresee which links will be needed. For example, a photocopier repair manual will usually be accessed by a reader because the photocopier is exhibiting various symptoms. Links between questions about symptoms and potential causes can be made by the author on the basis of an understanding of the machinery and an appreciation of the reader's purpose.

Where the text is an encyclopædia and the reader may have a wide variety of purposes, the nature of the linkages is far from obvious (See Chapter 5, Glasgow Online) and will often revert to simple keyword jumps. For example, in an information node relating to giraffes, mention of 'Africa' will allow the reader to jump to an information node concerning Africa.

We have earlier made the point that read-only documents place the onus on the author to provide appropriate links. However, the second market development described above, the move to large electronic documents on CD-ROM, also suggests that the author needs to think carefully about the range of tasks for which the document might be used and to provide appropriate links. A large document offers proportionally more scope for not finding specific information than a small document.

If the author can foresee a range of tasks and provide 'templates' to support these tasks, then the reader is more likely to interact successfully with the document. Such a template would be a means of reducing the data available, a means of selective display of information or what Conklin refers to as 'information filtering techniques'. This does not mean that pure unguided browsing need not be possible, rather that it not be offered as the default mode.

A document taxonomy

The foregoing leads us to suggest that what is required is an understanding of the types of document which can be adequately represented via electronic media. We assume that the various types will map onto various purposes for which the documents are used, which in turn should lead to suggestions for the overall structure of linkages required to support such purposes. We are currently engaged in an experimental investigation of such a taxonomy, but we present some of the background discussion below.

The range of types of paper documents currently available is quite considerable: newspapers, magazines, paperback novels, journals, textbooks, reference books, maps and software manuals are just a few that spring readily to mind.

Although it is often said that hypertext frees the information from the linear form of the printed page, it is clear that for certain types of document such freedom is neither necessary nor indeed desirable. For example, the detective novel is clearly a literary form which relies heavily on the linear format; a philosophical argument frequently builds from earlier arguments in such a way that it would not be appropriate to jump into the middle without having encountered the earlier material; mathematical theorems may require the building of parallel strands before the final proof, but the strands are logically prior to the proof and therefore some degree of linearity is inevitable.

On the other hand, a psychology textbook is frequently arranged in chapters which treat different sub-areas, and the nature of the subject matter is so interconnected that the final arrangement of chapters is somewhat arbitrary. Incidentally, the fact that hypertext systems readily support such non-linear text should not be taken to imply that only non-linear texts are appropriately contained in hypertext systems. Similarly, the fact that certain paper documents are traditionally seen as being linear (eg the alphabetical list in the telephone directory) should not be taken to imply that they could not be adequately represented as a hypertext.

One possible approach to determining structure, particularly applicable where a paper document is being converted to hypertext format, is to study a group of users interacting with the paper document. This enables the electronic version to be structured in a manner best suited to the way in which it is likely to be used. We have adopted this approach recently in order to inform the building of a large, full-text database of journal articles in hypertext format. An analysis of readers' interactions with scientific journals was carried out in order to identify the type of structure that would best support their use (Dillon *et al*, 1988). The results indicate that journal articles are rarely read in a serial fashion. Readers, all of whom were professional research workers, tended to overlook much of the contents, particularly the Method and Results sections of experimental papers. The typical interaction involved browsing the Introduction, scanning the section headings and then browsing the Discussion. More detailed study of the article might only occur if the reader's task required a thorough grasp of the contents. Such results suggest, therefore, that the hypertext structure for a journal article should be very different from the paper version. In general terms, care should be taken not to assume that the structure inherent in the paper document is the optimum structure to support the reader's task.

The 'repair manual' type of text would seem to fall easily into the hierarchical form which Guide produces with ease. The top level can contain the various sections (eg fuel, electrics, bodywork and so forth in a car maintenance manual), each section being linked to more detailed text and graphics. This form of organization still allows for links between sections, acknowledging that a car's operation involves the topics of several sections working together. However, placing the information in the global structure of a hierarchy means that the reader can more quickly access the information relevant to a particular task (eg 'How do I change the spark plugs?').

The encyclopædia type of text seems to encourage a relatively 'flat' structure with linking via keywords, probably because the material is so general that it is very difficult to anticipate the precise task for which it will be used. Even so, systems like HyperTIES provide levels of the same information; if the user moves the cursor to a selectable word a one-line explanation appears at the bottom of the screen along with an option to jump to a complete node devoted to the topic. It should be remembered that such systems still require the author to make decisions regarding which topics to provide complete nodes for.

These are just a few examples of global structures which perhaps best suit particular kinds of document and task. They are not the only possibilities and we hope our research will provide a range of useful structures and some guidelines concerning the tasks to which they are best suited.

Our experiences

As part of our work relating to the reading and manipulation of electronic documents we have been involved in the construction of various hypertext documents for demonstration and experimental purposes. We were initially concerned with problems of navigation and manipulation and with the comparison of the use of paper and electronic versions of the same document, in addition to comparing the same document implemented on different electronic systems with different interfaces. We have also seen various other demonstration hypertext documents.

When translating a document from paper to electronic form many of the problems we have raised above do not really occur. Putting the AppleTalk manual into the format of a Guide document presents few problems because the structure already inherent in the paper form is a reasonable one for the tasks to be performed by the reader. Similarly, implementing a TIES demonstration database in Guide or HyperCard is time-consuming but not difficult. It is possibly because many of the existing hypertext documents have been built by 'porting' reasonable paper documents that the authoring problems have not achieved greater prominence

However, we have also seen a variety of problems arising out of the origination of documents in the various hypertext systems. The three most common problems are: (a) links to nodes which do not exist; (b) nodes which are not linked at all and are therefore inaccessible; and (c) nodes which are inadvertently linked to themselves. In cases (a) and (c) the result depends on how 'fault-tolerant' the system is. Case (b) is quite difficult to spot unless the system is automatically producing a map of nodes or the author leaves the authoring level and browses at the system or file level. As Brown (1988) has pointed out, there is a general requirement for tools for 'testing and validation'.

These are perhaps somewhat trivial problems — the equivalent of referring to an author and then omitting to provide the appropriate reference, or including references with no corresponding mention in the text. Editors will attest to the prevalence of such errors even from experienced authors. More important is the decision-making required by the author in providing information or ideas and making the appropriate links. Traditional publishers limit the size of books for sound economic reasons and in accordance with market forces. With the power of modern packages and the capacity of even microcomputer-based systems, there is a temptation to continue adding information and links for no better reason than the fact that the space is available.

The experience we all have in writing paper documents is complemented by the even greater experience of reading and manipulating such documents. In the same manner that we need to replace our paper reading and manipulation skills with appropriate electronic equivalents, so we need to learn new authoring skills if we are to achieve the potential of hypertext. Our research into document taxonomies may provide suggestions for appropriate global structures, but it will not free the author of the responsibility for providing the microstructure required by the reader.

Conclusions

The authoring of read-only hypertext documents requires considerable effort on the part of the author if the readers' task is to be adequately supported. This effort takes the form of decision-making regarding the nature of the linkages provided in the text. While particular macrostructures may be appropriate for particular kinds of texts, the author will need to anticipate the needs of the reader if the document is to be used successfully.

We therefore need to understand better the uses to which documents are put, and possibly even to provide decision support systems for authoring. Such considerations are properly the concern of the Human Factors community and should not be left by default to the programmer or system designer. While it is commonplace to argue for a user-centred approach to design, we should remember that the initial user of a hypertext system is the author, not the reader.

References

Archer D, Rawsthorn S and Robinson B (1987) CD-ROM: the technology and its applications. Report #Hat/a/40. School of Engineering, The Hatfield Polytechnic, Hatfield, Herts.

Brown P J (1986) Interactive documentation. *Software — Practice and Experience* 16 (3): 291-9.

Brown P J (1988) Hypertext: the way forward. In: *Proceedings of EP88*. Edited by van Vliet J C. Cambridge University Press, Cambridge.

Bush V (1945) As we may think. *Atlantic Monthly*, July. pp 101-8.

Conklin J (1987) Hypertext: an introduction and survey. *IEEE Computer* 21 (9): 17-41.

Dillon A, Richardson J and McKnight C (1988) Towards the design of a full-text searchable database: implications from a study of journal usage. *British Journal of Academic Librarianship*. In press.

Engelbart D C (1963) A conceptual framework for the augmentation of man's intellect. In: *Vistas in Information Handling*, Volume 1. Spartan Books, London.

Marchionini G and Shneiderman B (1988) Finding facts vs browsing knowledge in hypertext systems. *IEEE Computer*, January. pp 70-9.

Morariu J and Shneiderman B (1986) Design and research on The Interactive Encyclopedia System (TIES). *Proceedings of 29th Conference of the Association for the Development of Computer Based Instructional Systems*. pp19-21.

Nelson T H (1967) Getting it out of our system. In: *Information Retrieval: A Critical Review*. Edited by Schechter G. Thompson Books, Washington DC.

Nelson T H (1988) Managing immense storage. *Byte*, January. pp 225-38.

Walker J H (1988) Supporting document development with Concordia. *IEEE Computer*, January. pp 48-59.

Yankelovich N, Meyrowitz N and van Dam An (1985) Reading and writing the electronic book. *IEEE Computer*, October. pp 15-29.

Notes

[1]   This work was supported by the British Library Research and Development Department and the OCLC Online Computer Library Centre, Dublin, Ohio.

10

Graham Storrs
The Alvey DHSS large demonstrator project Knowledge ANalysis Tool: KANT

Abstract
KANT is a knowledge analysis tool that has been developed as part of an Alvey collaborative project. The application has been for the Department of Health and Social Security in the UK. KANT supports procedures for knowledge analysis to facilitate the translation of paper source into hypertext.

Introduction
The Alvey DHSS Large Demonstrator Project is a £7 million, five year research project aimed at demonstrating the viability of intelligent decision support for large, legislation-based organizations. It is a collaborative project, partially funded by the UK Government, between Logica Cambridge, ICL, the Universities of Lancaster, Liverpool and Surrey, Imperial College and the Department of Health and Social Security (DHSS).[1]

The project is building three applications as demonstrator systems. These are:

- **The Claimant Information System:** this will provide advice and explanations to potential claimants of social security benefits as to their eligibility to claim and the consequences of claims they might make.

- **The Local Office System:** this is intended to provide decision support for DHSS adjudication officers who are assessing claims for benefits in local offices. These people are legally empowered adjudicators and the decisions they must make are affected by large bodies of complex legislation and case law.

- **The Policy System:** this will provide support for DHSS policy makers. The job of a policy maker is to formulate, explain and monitor the policy of the department, to implement it as social security legislation and to modify existing legislation so as to reflect the current policy.

Knowledge analysis in the DHSS demonstrator project

One of the prime objectives of the project is to investigate the use of very large knowledge bases. So it is with the local office (LO) system that we will be particularly concerned in this paper as it is only within this application that a very large knowledge base is being built.

While the project is faced with many problems of how to represent and organize very large bodies of knowledge within a machine for efficient inference, it rapidly became clear that the major difficulties with building large knowledge bases were in the analysis of the knowledge, the validation and verification of the knowledge base and the maintenance of the knowledge base. This is so despite the fact that the sources of knowledge for the systems we are building are, on the face of it, highly structured, definitional and rule-like.

A style of knowledge analysis has developed within the LO application. This is based on a restructuring of the knowledge in the various sources (Adjudication Officer's Guide - AOG - and the Acts and Regulations) into an essentially hierarchical breakdown of the concepts involved (eg. the notion of 'capital' in Income Support). Onto these, the 'operation' of the regulations is superimposed as a set of linking rules and this 'legal' perspective of the knowledge is systematically mapped to another structured knowledge base which represents the users' conceptions and the 'task' knowledge. The task knowledge is unlike the legal knowledge in that part of it must be acquired through techniques such as interviews and simulations, but most of it is also contained in the AOG.

It is very difficult to say how large a 'very large knowledge base' is as there are no adequate metrics. The target we have set ourselves is to have encoded about one-third of the printed source material required for the adjudication of claims for Income Support (in fact, the project expects to have about half the source material encoded). This should encompass about two volumes of the eleven-volume AOG plus all the relevant acts and regulations as well as parts of some other sources (eg. the Child Poverty Action Group handbook). Readers unfamiliar with these sources will not necessarily appreciate how large, how dense or how densely cross-referenced this body of knowledge is.

It is the cross-referencing in particular that leads to extreme difficulties for the knowledge analyst. We have estimated that in a typical month's work each analyst will have referred to approximately 20 megabytes of text as a result of reference-following. This is a rather extreme instance of the 'thumbs problem' and it is simply not possible for a person to keep track of this information unaided.

The requirements for KANT

In order to support the knowledge analysis activity within the LO application, a hypertext-based tool, known as KANT, has been built. The requirements for KANT were:

- to directly support the project's knowledge analysis style - that is, to support the procedures for knowledge analysis that the present analysts are familiar with;

- to be usable by the present analysts - these are people with a legal or systems background without, necessarily, any computer skills;

- to be able to allow the user to work on more than one analysis at the same time;

- to have a sensible and, as far as possible, automatic route from paper source to KANT form;

- to be able to cope with the anticipated volume of material to be analysed - this involves having multiple sources (eg. several acts plus the AOG) available at the same time;

- to handle this quantity of text without slowing down the analysis - we took this to mean that browsing the sources should be able to be done at a pace similar to that of turning and scanning printed pages and that retrieving a reference by following a link should bring up the target text within a second;

- that the sources should look, as nearly as possible, identical to their paper equivalents (a requirement imposed by our users which caused great difficulties).

The Knowledge ANalysis Tool (KANT)

Most of the design of KANT (and, indeed, most of the slog of turning paper sources into KANT sources) has been done by Chris Burton at ICL and the implementation was done largely by Nick Perry, also at ICL. The implemented system is written in Interlisp and LOOPS on a Xerox 1186 Lisp workstation and makes extensive use of the project's screen management and text management software tools in order to gain the necessary performance.

KANT will allow the analyst to open up as many source documents as are needed. These each reside in a separate window and the windows may be moved, shaped, buried and revealed as suits the user. Sources in the context of the DHSS Large Demonstrator are such things as legislation, procedures guidelines and case law manuals. Sources may be browsed by scrolling at the rate of a line, paragraph, or page, or they may be searched for occurrences of strings. Similarly, the user may open as many 'structure' windows as necessary. These contain the results of the analysis. For each session, each node of each structure has 'provenance' data attached. This gives the name of the analyst who has working on it, the reason for the analysis, the date and the time and a full record of all the significant changes to the node. Provenance records may be reviewed or printed as desired.

The structures created by the analyst are basically hierarchical and are displayed as indented blocks of text (our users prefer text to graphical displays). Structures may be folded and unfolded in the style of 'ideas processors' or 'outliners'. Each node has its own internal structure. It has a title, a body of free text and a rules section (for adding rules in an 'intermediate' rule language). A node may be moved to a new location within the same structure or copied to another location in the same or a different structure (in all cases bringing all its subordinate nodes and maintaining all its links appropriately).

We have found that analysts like to work with several source documents open and several analysis structures open at the same time. Interestingly, some of these structures may be used as 'scratch-pads' recording progress in the analysis and adding commentary and annotation to work in progress.

Nodes in the structure may have links attached to them. These links may go either to a piece of text in a source document, to nodes in another structure, or to other nodes in the same structure. The links may be followed by buttoning on them and doing so reveals the target text or node almost immediately (ie. with a sub-second response time). The links may be named by the analyst and it is found that for each analyst, analyses proceed with relatively small numbers of link types (ie. around 10). However, different analysts use different sets of link types and have commented that shared sets and standard common subsets might be useful additions to the system.

KANTification

The process of taking text and moving it into the KANT format has, inevitably, become known as KANTification and it is a non-trivial problem. To give us the speed we need from the system, we handle text in blocks rather than character by character. These blocks must be pre-defined for the system. They are, typically, about the size of a paragraph of text but may range in size from a full page to a single character. They not only include text from the body of sources but also marginal notes, footnotes and cross-references.

The materials from which we cull our knowledge are occasionally found on magnetic tape in a standard mark-up language such as SGML. Such languages have sufficient information in them for us to specify the rules of KANTification and apply them to get a KANTified text. Some of the material is available on floppy disc (in more or less obscure formats). The process in this case usually requires some manual intervention to ensure that the word processor conventions are correctly interpreted as properly formatted KANT text blocks (in particular the handling of footnotes and marginal notes can be problematic). However, a great deal of the sources we must deal with exist only in paper form. Using optical character reading followed by manual formatting has proved successful but tedious and expensive. A more cost-effective technique has been to have a word-processing bureau retype the documents and mark them up as they enter them according to our specifications.

User experiences

Several of our analysts in the LO application (and, increasingly, in Policy and Claimant Information) have now used KANT in their work. The feedback from them has been largely positive. The major objective of using such a hypertext system to solve the 'thumbs problem' has been met to judge by their reports. Problems with the system are largely to do with surface HCI features rather than the users' conceptual model or the system's support for the task.

One interesting observation is that users find they occasionally have difficulty in navigating around large analysis structures that they have created. The feeling seems to be that the physical appearance of the indented text blocks they create is more homogeneous than normal text so the usual cues to location are not present - even though the structures are strictly hierarchical. We do not yet have a solution to this problem but users have solved it by adding ancillary structures linked to their analyses which act as guides or indexes and this may be the best general solution. We also intend to provide a graphical overview of the structure on which will be indicated the user's current location. This overview will serve the additional function of allowing the user to move rapidly to another part of the structure.

A more easily remedied problem is that some analysts have asked for the ability to create links and annotations within the source documents themselves. This is a facility much discussed in the hypertext literature, but was not one which emerged as a requirement during the design of KANT. Our suspicion is that it is a possibility which only became apparent to users after they had already gained some experience with hypertext.

Another interesting finding, already referred to, is that the analysts tend to create and use a relatively small number of link types. Some of these are for the object-level analysis of the source and others are for meta-level comment and structuring of the analysis process itself. Analysts seem to believe that a pre-defined set of links could be a useful addition to the system even though they tend to invent quite different sets for themselves. Such a set of links would, in effect, provide a basic epistemology of the domain and it is interesting to speculate how these sets of links might differ from domain to domain, how they might be employed in a distributed group analysis process in order to provide consistency in the analysis and how their semantics might be defined for the system in order to provide a deeper understanding of the resulting structures and greater machine assistance with the analysis process.

Legislation is constantly changing. In particular the so-called secondary legislation (regulations) may be changing very rapidly. There is therefore a need to be able to update sources as they change, maintaining all the links that previously existed, adding new links (doing new analysis) where appropriate, and ensuring that changes in the source are reflected in the analysis and therefore the knowledge base. Given the organization in KANT of a source document into a 'pool' of KANTified paragraphs, the document the user sees ('virtual documents') have an actual internal existence as ordered lists of references to the paragraphs in the pool. This provides the basis for the flexibility needed in the structure of a source document to support the maintenance of extensive and constantly changing material. Changes to a document are usually notified as a (sometimes very long) list of paragraphs which should be added to it or which replace existing paragraphs in it. To create a new version of a document, these new paragraphs must be added to the pool and a new virtual document created which is like the old one except that the new paragraphs replace or extend the old ones. Any hypertext links which existed for paragraphs in the old document which are no longer present in the new one must then either be appropriately connected to the replacing paragraph or deleted. The changes will be easily traceable through to the analyses and any other changes can be propagated all the way through to the knowledge base. What is more, as old paragraphs are not deleted from the pool and retain their original links, the old virtual document can be retained and thus a complete system of version control is possible.

The choice of the size of the node is an interesting parameter to consider. KANT takes the position that each node is a 'paragraph'. This designation is more to support the users' conceptual model than it is accurate. A paragraph may indeed be a paragraph (in a source text for instance), but it may also be a footnote, a marginal note, or whatever. It may even be a single character if that is appropriate. However, in the analysis structures, the 'paragraphs' are always structured. At present, the structure has three parts that the user sees, title, text and rule, each of which has a different meaning to the system. Facilities will soon exist for the user to define his or her own node structures as well as there being several other 'library' structures available

The choice of the paragraph as the 'grain size' for the node has some consequences. For instance, some users have expressed the need to link to and from individual phrases within paragraphs and individual components of rules. The fact that this is not allowed sometimes leads them to create unnatural structures, breaking up their analysis in awkward ways so that the linkable chunks are each in a separate node.

Other systems tackle the grain size problem in different ways. The card-based systems, for example, generally use a whole card as the unit for linking to, while they allow single words or smaller units to be used to link from. Such choices seem to lead to different perceptions of the systems being used. Certainly there is something of the feel of using menus - albeit menus embedded in text - with the card-based systems, whereas text-oriented systems such as KANT retain much more of the feeling of reading linear text. In fact, rather as there is a continuum between hypertext and semantic networks, there is one between hypertext and menu systems. In this case, the dimensions which vary are; the size of the displayable unit (ie. what constitutes the display of a linked-to node), the explicitness of the marking of links in the text, and the amount of embedding of the linked text in non-linked text.

Concluding remarks

Some of the most exciting and, indeed, appropriate applications for hypertext systems appear to be in areas to do with creativity, exploration and design. Knowledge analysis is clearly such an area and the hypertext system we have built to support this activity within the DHSS Demonstrator Project is proving to be an effective and useful tool, apparently well-liked by the project's analysts and well targeted to their needs.

The use of KANT takes us only so far down the road towards a finished knowledge base. That is, it takes us as far as an intermediate representation of the rules and structures we wish to incorporate. Another tool, the Knowledge Base Builder (KBB) is then used for knowledge encoders to take the KANT intermediate representation and turn it into rules and objects in the target knowledge representation language. Explorations are in progress to discover the extent to which the two tools can be merged into a single environment for analysing knowledge and building knowledge bases. One great advantage of such a system would be the fact that individual knowledge base entities could then be traced back all the way to the original sources with a clear 'audit trail', provenance information and records of intermediate development decisions. For applications based on legal sources which are constantly being revised, this traceability would be of enormous benefit to those tasked with the maintenance of the knowledge base.

Another interesting aspect to the development of a hypertext tool for knowledge analysis is that there appears to be a smooth progression between hypertext and some knowledge representation schemes which is potentially exploitable.

Hypertext, in its simplest form, is a set of nodes connected together by undifferentiated links. Each node is an unstructured piece of text or graphics (or both) and each link is a unidirectional association between two nodes. However, both nodes and links could have a lot more structure than this and their structure could have a lot more meaning for the system. For instance, the nodes need not be free text but could be structured so that there were a number of named text, graphics or even numeric 'fields'. The nodes could also be of different types. The links too need not be simple associations but could be special types of relationship such as 'is defined by' or 'supersedes'. There could also be meta-level organization so that link relationships could be described in terms of their directionality, or their transitivity (a link type such as 'supersedes' would be unidirectional and transitive, for instance).

In fact, as nodes and links become more and more structured and more and more meaningful, the nature of the system changes progressively from being hypertext to being a kind of knowledge representation style known as a semantic network. The best-known semantic network representations are those supported by the popular artificial intelligence (AI) toolkits such as Art, Kee, and KnowledgeCraft. These representations are also known as frame-based because the node is a 'frame', that is, a set of labelled and, perhaps, typed slots for information - rather like a record in conventional programming languages. Some of these slots may hold a reference to another frame and thus become, effectively, relationships (ie. links) between nodes.

Thus we have a continuum between hypertext and knowledge representation schemes which varies along the two dimensions of node and link structure. The existence of this continuum makes possible the opportunity to build intelligence into hypertext systems. The way to do this would be to add sufficient structure to both nodes and links so that the hypertext 'document' may be interpreted as knowledge by a knowledge-based system.

Notes

[1]   This work was carried out as part of the DHSS Large Demonstrator Project, supported by the Alvey Directorate and the UK Science and Engineering Research Council. The collaborators are ICL, Logica, Imperial College, and the universities of Lancaster, Liverpool and Surrey. The DHSS is also actively participating. The assistance of other project members is gratefully acknowledged. The views expressed here are those of the author.

11

Elizabeth B Duncan
A faceted approach to hypertext?

Abstract
Hypertext is a 'technology' which can be exploited to utilize some basic principles in information science, such as facet analysis, to structure knowledge. Knowledge bases built on the principles outlined below, using hypertext, will help users to explore information in a more flexible way than is possible with conventional text.

Introduction

Hypertext is a system of knowledge representation in which elements of knowledge can be assembled in different ways according to the different perspectives of users of the system. In computer terms this means that a hypertext system can be both dynamic and interactive in a way that linear text can not - the user can explore a knowledge base in ways not previously determined by the system. At a recent conference of the HCI Group of the British Computer Society, Monk *et al* (1988 % definition)[1] described hypertext as:

> '*removing some of the constraints of conventional linear text by providing mechanisms for physically realizing the conceptual links between related sections of material*'.

Facet analysis

In information science, the concept of assembling ideas at a retrieval stage rather than at a storage stage of the information search process, ie. in a post-coordinate rather than a pre-coordinate mode, is well known. (see Foskett, 1988 % background). Combining post-coordination of ideas with a more flexible approach to classification (formal or otherwise) in the form of facet analysis, rather than hierarchical division, provides a structure which allows users to both explore and create new combinations of ideas, not previously determined by the system.

The basic principle of facet analysis is that concepts can be grouped using a characteristic of division which is not necessarily hierarchical. In other words, subjects which have previously been subdivided by progressive hierarchical arrangement, forming the familiar 'tree structures' of conventional indexing theory, can be looked on as patterns of horizontal division as well as vertical divisions. In any area of complex ideas there are difficulties in accommodating subjects comfortably into one or other subject division and by using horizontal groupings, new subjects are formed. Information theorists interested in structuring knowledge for the purpose of clarifying understandings recognized this horizontal grouping as recurring 'facets' or planes of understanding (Ranganathan, 1965 % background) and defined the term facet analysis as the process by which a subject is analysed based on this principle.

So, for instance, the 'sociology' or 'historical development' of science could be studied in relation to the 'sociology' or 'historical development' of other subjects. At a simpler level, a cat can be studied either as a mammal with four legs and therefore in a similar class to a dog, or it can be seen as having a role in the rehabilitation of mentally ill patients alongside other forms of therapy. Foskett (1988 % example) describes the method of classifying a document using this principle as follows:

> '*categories (of index terms) are derived from the main subject or class by a series of characteristics which are each logically distinct from the other, and which can be clearly seen to be based on the logic inherent in the main subject ...the main process in classifying a document is therefore in a post-coordinate mode ... assembling those terms from the different facets of the scheme.*'

Facet analysis and hypertext

The ideas behind the process of facet analysis have parallells in linguistic theory and it is a combination of facet and semantic analyses which should form the basis of our exploitation of hypertext technology. Vickery (1986 % explanation) compares the semantic model of human memory structures used by Lindsay and Norman (1977 % detail % definition) with the analysis of subjects by facet used by himself and others in subject classification.

Lindsay and Norman described 'roles which characterize parts of an event' as:

Action
Agent
Conditional
Instrument
Location
Object
Purpose
Quality
Recipient
Time

These correspond closely with some of the facets defined by Vickery (1986 % definition) as being useful within a science and technology classification:

Attributes
Object
Parts
Place
Processes
Properties
Substances
Time

All of these categories can be regarded as ways of looking at subjects from different perspectives, eg. looking at mathematics as it has developed over time, or at a motor car either from the point of view of what it is made up of (*Parts*) or of what it is designed to do (*Object*).

The relevance of this thinking to hypertext is that we have in the non-linearity of the hypertext approach a way of allowing the post-coordination of ideas which will enable a user to look at a subject from different points of view. Using a hypertext system such as NoteCards, we are able to define concepts as being part of more than one hierarchy by 'filing' reference to them under different headings. The hypertext nature of NoteCards allows regrouping of the same knowledge from different perspectives by the user, in exactly the same way in which facet analysis is understood to operate.

Knowledge elicitation

Research based on facet analysis theory (McAleese and Duncan, 1988 % results) has been able to define facets which may be labelled differently in different subject domains, but which are essentially transferable.

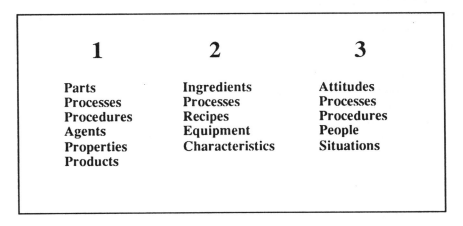

1	2	3
Parts	Ingredients	Attitudes
Processes	Processes	Processes
Procedures	Recipes	Procedures
Agents	Equipment	People
Properties	Characteristics	Situations
Products		

Fig 1 *Facet labels - Column 1 = generic labelling, Column 2 = catering, Column 3 = social skills/counselling.*

Fig 1 illustrates, for example, what label the general facet descriptors (Column 1) might be given when used in either a hard skills area (Catering, Column 2) or a soft skills area (Counselling, Column 3).

The examples above are taken from knowledge bases built for research purposes, using the hypertext system 'NoteCards' on a Xerox 1186 workstation (McAleese and Duncan, 1987 % detail). The hypertext principle allows an expert to 'throw down' ideas randomly, while talking about a subject, knowing that they can develop each thread independently, linking them together at a later stage. Various devices, such as graphical browsers, can give a global view as they progress, and can highlight inadequacies or inconsistencies in the knowledge base as it is being built up. The knowledge base consists of elements of textual, graphical or video information, linked by differing forms of relationship.

One of the helpful structures developed to assist in the aim for completeness of knowledge acquisition, however, has been the idea of facets. Using FileBoxes to simulate facet categories, experts are able to 'file' or group chunks of knowledge associated with different aspects of their expertise. In addition the same elements can be stored in different fileboxes (ie. facets). This is equivalent, both for the expert and the user, to looking at their subject from different perspectives. In the case of the expert, the facet label (eg. Processes, Products) acts as a stimulus for the generation of related concepts, at the same time forming a structure visible to a user. Further, if each facet type is associated with its own template and icon style, they could be recognized as forming a rough 'grammar' of a subject area. A 'sentence', for instance, could be constructed by suggesting the combination of a term from one facet followed by one from a different facet, joined by a particular link type, as in Fig 2.

{Agents} *<causing>* {Processes}

Fig 2 *Basis of machine 'grammar' based on recognition of facet types.*

Using a tool kit of facets and links in this way, a 'reasoning system' can be constructed. In our exploitation of some of the above ideas using NoteCards for the elicitation and representation of knowledge, several interesting questions have arisen, namely:

- what are the 'generic' or universally identifiable facets?

- is it possible to rename them satisfactorily in all subject domains?

- is the principle more useful in some domains (eg. in hard skills areas) than in others?

- does the 'machine grammar' work for users?

We have gone a little way along the road to answering some of these questions in the two files referred to so far. Future research will apply these to other subject domains. Hypertext allows us the technology with which to experiment on applying structures to knowledge which will be helpful and flexible to a user.

References

Duncan E B and McAleese R (1982) Qualified citations on-line? In: *National On-line Meeting Proceedings*, Learned Information. Edited by Williams M. New York.

Foskett D J (1988) Information classification and retrieval. In: *Encyclopaedia of Educational Media Communications and Technology*, 2nd Edition. Edited by Unwin D J and McAleese R. Greenwood Press.

Lindsay P H and Norman D A (1977) *Human information Processing*, 2nd edition. Academic Press, New York.

McAleese R and Duncan E B (1987) The graphical representation of 'terrain' and 'street' knowledge in an interface to a database system. In: *On-Line Information '87*, 11th International On-line Meeting, Learned Information.

McAleese R and Duncan E B (1988) Alvey Project MMI/110 Cognitive Workshop Report, 23-24 June 1988. Project Number 00134. (Unpub).

Monk A F, Walsh P and Dix A J (1988) A comparison of hypertext scrolling and folding as mechanisms for program browsing. In: *People and Computers IV*. Edited by Jones D M and Winder R. Cambridge University Press, Cambridge.

Ranganathan S R (1965) The colon classification. In: *The Intellectual Organisation of Knowledge*. Edited by Artandi S. Rutgers University.

Vickery B C (1986) Knowledge representation: a brief review. *Journal of Documentation* 42 (3): 145-59.

Notes

[1]   Citations in this chapter have been qualified in line with research carried out by Duncan and McAleese (1982 %expansion).

12

M R Kibby[1]
J T Mayes

Towards intelligent hypertext

Abstract

StrathTutor, a hypertext system designed for tutoring applications, is described. The system has a routing algorithm based on work by Hintzman on human memory that facilitates the user in making jumps for one frame to another. The routing algorithm which is based on attributes and pattern matching is described.

Introduction

Hypertext is widely accepted as an important step forward in information storage and presentation. However, it and hypermedia systems in general, are also recognized as being in an early stage of development and various workers have pointed out deficiencies in current implementations and possible problems which may be encountered when large systems are generated (see Hardman,1988). Among these are problems for the user in navigation, or of getting 'lost in hyperspace', (see Chapter 7) and of retrieving material, particularly that already known to the user. Many such problems may be ameliorated by the introduction of intelligent hypertext, directed towards providing intelligent tools for both the creator and the user. We are doubtful whether the present exclusively manual methods for creating the links between elements of hypertext will prove to be viable. Such links are more restrictive than the keywords used in many computer-based bibliographies; they present barriers to the exploration of hyperspace and are cumbersome to introduce and to manage even in small systems. They will become a limiting factor, ultimately to be rejected, in generating large hypertext systems such as the Xanadu project (Nelson, 1988) or the Glasgow Online project (Baird and Percival, see Chapter 5), for the same reasons that unstructured programming has been rejected by the computing community.

The work we report here has been directed towards finding appropriate methods for the automatic computation of 'relatedness' between nodes in hypertext, of conceptual connectivity or semantic proximity. We thus envisage large hypertext systems in which the activation of a node (a fragment of text, a frame, a screen) will take the user automatically to the most appropriate node without the need for the link between the two nodes ever to have been explicitly coded.

Our approach was first influenced by work in a rather different area, that of the modelling of human memory. Our implementation of the ideas incorporated in this approach into an interactive learning system has a plausibility about it that is probably quite spurious. There is no particular reason why a learning-by-browsing system (the system we have so far developed) should be any more effective for having knowledge retrieval mechanisms that work the same way as those inside the learner's head. Nevertheless, since human memory is certainly the largest, most complex and most interconnected knowledge base that we know, it seems reasonable that successful modelling of that system will yield valuable insights into the problem of how most effectively to represent and retrieve knowledge in large hypertext systems.

MINERVA: Hintzman's simulation model of human memory

Given the following assumptions, most of the theoretical distinctions that have dominated the recent history of memory research, such as the dichotomies of episodic and semantic memory or of primary and secondary memory, simply fall out. These assumptions can be stated as follows:

(a) *Only episodic traces are stored in memory.* There is no distinction between episodic memory, the storing of individual experiences and semantic memory, for abstract concepts. All information, however general, is retrieved from the pool of episodic traces.

(b) *Repetition produces multiple traces of an item.* The human memory system is assumed to be a vast collection of episodic traces, each of which is a record of an experience. Repeated experiences are recorded as separate traces. Thus learning becomes a matter of redundancy rather than the strengthening of particular pathways.

(c) *A retrieval cue contacts all memory traces simultaneously.* The memory system is interrogated by presenting a retrieval cue or 'probe' which is simultaneously matched with every trace.

(d) *Each trace is activated according to its similarity to the retrieval cue.*

(e) *All traces respond in parallel, the retrieved information reflecting their summed output.* The echo that is returned from the probe represents the summed reactions of all traces. Individual memory traces cannot be located and examined in isolation. Since a trace's contribution to the echo is determined by its degree of activation, it is only those that are relatively similar to the probe that make a significant contribution to the echo.

Hintzman (1984, 1986) described a computational model that seemed to us to offer not only a radical approach to solving some of the problems of modelling human memory but also an approach to the problem of content-addressable retrieval from large knowledge bases in general. In fact, as Hintzman points out, this approach had first been described almost 80 years ago in the memory theory of the psychologist, Richard Semon (1923). The basic idea is that all activated memory traces respond in parallel during retrieval. Abstract ideas will arise when individual traces having common properties are activated by the same retrieval cue. Semon argued that the contents of consciousness are produced by a kind of resonant state (homophony), in which the distinctive features of the activated memory traces mutually interfere. Thus the shared properties of all such traces will stand out or 'resonate'. Hintzman's contribution has been to cast this theory into the form of a computer model, MINERVA, and to show that it is capable of simulating many of the known properties of human memory.

The success of this model is particularly impressive because it requires only a few simple ideas. From these relatively simple ideas Hintzman constructs his computational model. An experience or event is represented as a trace or vector, an ordered list of features or attributes. He uses a three-state attribute system: the attribute is present, present in a negated form, or not-present represented by the values +1, -1, or 0 respectively. For example a trace or the probe could be a large vector, vi, where:

$$vi = (1\ 0\ \text{-}1 \ldots \text{-}1\ 1\ 0 \ldots 0\ 0\ 1)$$

For each retrieval, an index of similarity is computed between the probe and each trace. Each trace is then activated by a weighted function of its similarity to the probe, wi. The echo, e, is computed by summing all weighted traces:

$$e = \sum wi\ vi$$

It has both intensity and content. The intensity of the echo reflects in part the number of traces matching the probe. Thus multiple representations, the redundancy built in by repetition of experience, directly produce an echo of greater intensity. The content, on the other hand, is the pattern of attributes that is returned after the matching of the probe against all individual traces. The echo therefore comprises a kind of profile or histogram across features or attributes encoded in the traces.

MINERVA succeeds in simulating the memory characteristics of associative recall and schema abstraction. Only traces that are similar to the probe become activated. Nevertheless, those traces will contain information not present in the probe itself and this gives rise to associative retrieval. A general concept emerges from the probing of MINERVA's traces by a kind of 'resonance', not by the storing of an abstracted representation. How a concept emerges will vary according to which episodic traces have been activated by the probe; the process is highly context-specific. The system is able to retrieve an abstracted prototype of the category when cued with a category name and to retrieve a category name when cued with a category exemplar.

Attributes and pattern matching

'The useful capacity of memory for patterned information depends on its ability to recall the wanted items with sufficient selectivity... Associative recall ought to take into account some form of the concept of similarity' (Kohonen,1987). The use of attributes for retrieving information therefore depends on measures of similarity, proximity, or semantic distance.

Hintzman used a three-state attribute system. He was partly concerned with the phenomenon of loss of memory elements and clearly placed value on the not-present state as distinct from the negated form. We have been unable to justify the use of the negated attribute in our application. Furthermore, using a two-state system simplifies both the storage and manipulation of attributes in practice. In the development of our reactive learning system, we have experimented with various measures of relatedness which exhibit different characteristics in use. Some are true measures of similarity (S), others measure dissimilarity (D). To some extent the choice is arbitrary, based on experience and previous practice. In the examples to be given we consider two vectors of attributes x and y, where the individual elements are 0 (attribute not-present) or 1 (attribute present), easily represented by just one bit. The function bitcount counts the number of bits which have the value 1 in the vector, and not, and, and or are the usual logical connectives.

Hamming distance

This function is equivalent to counting bits in the exclusive-or of the two vectors. As it stands it is dependent on the length of vectors being compared but if these are all of the same length that is irrelevant.

$$D = bitcount ((not\ x\ and\ y)\ or\ (x\ and\ not\ y))$$

Tanimoto similarity measure

In this function, the attributes are treated as members of a set, and simple set operations are carried out.

$$S = members\ (intersection\ of\ x\ and\ y)\ /\ members\ (union\ of\ x\ and\ y)$$

$$= bitcount\ (x\ and\ y)\ /\ bitcount\ (x\ or\ y)$$

where the function members counts the number of members in the specified set. The Tanimoto measure is independent of the length of the vectors. It has been found to behave well in practice and to be fast to compute.

Our similarity algorithm works only on content of the echo at the moment, although there is no reason in principle why it shouldn't be extended to include intensity as well. This could be done by giving each attribute a value, relating to its importance in the present frame.

Application to CAL: StrathTutor

We have taken the assumptions and some of the computational features of
Hintzman's model and applied them in a learning-by-browsing system on the
Macintosh, StrathTutor. (Mayes, Kibby and Watson, 1988). By representing
knowledge separately from the contents of instructional frames and by deferring
linkage until the link is required, StrathTutor exhibits some of the features
associated with intelligent systems.

Salient features of StrathTutor are:

- an information-free shell which makes full use of the already highly
  developed Macintosh user interface;

- authoring without programming and no coding at the level of the
  organization of the learning material. No links between frames explicitly
  represented and no sequencing necessary;

- knowledge represented as attributes. Up to 60 attributes used throughout a
  tutorial to code each frame of text and graphics;

- exploration of the frame base in a number of different ways;

- links computed at run time by pattern matching heuristics according to the
  type of interaction which the learner initiates.

- two types of computed link:
  - (i) selection of closest frame
  - (ii) selection of frame closest to the echo;

- self testing using quiz material generated via the knowledge base;

- feedback from the knowledge base to guide the learner on request;

- complete learner control.

Progress through the material is entirely a matter of choice by the learner.
Browsing in StrathTutor is largely conceptual; the learner is required continually
to search for links between frames at the level of the underlying concepts
(attributes).

StrathTutor is a small-scale implementation of what could be regarded as a
solution to the general problem of linking nodes in very large hypertext (or
hypermedia) systems. Hintzman's memory traces become multiple areas on each
frame denoted as 'hotspots', each hotspot having attached to it a subset of
attributes. Each frame can be represented as a profile of attributes, summed across
all hotspots in that frame. The 'probe' is generated by selecting a hotspot or a
menu item.

The advent of HyperCard for the Macintosh has presented us with a ready-
made opportunity to employ StrathTutor's heuristics in a novel environment.

There is the immediate prospect of making intelligent links in HyperCard between its cards and its stacks.

Discussion

StrathTutor demonstrates that fixed links between objects such as individual graphics or fragments of text are not necessary to generate a hypertext system. Moreover, we contend that removing fixed links provides a more flexible environment. During the development of our software, it became clear that as further ideas evolved for tools to support exploration by the learner, so they could be incorporated without drastic recoding, merely by reference to the knowledge base.

We do not suggest that all fixed links should be avoided. Indeed, StrathTutor has such links as part of its overall learning support environment. However, much useful structure will be implicit and many links may be generated using our approach that will be unanticipated by the author of the hypertext system.

A further potential advantage of the knowledge separation that we propose is that it becomes possible to have 'dynamic hypertext'. In our system each frame is separate, united with its underlying knowledge but independent of others until a link is formed at run time. A frame may be deleted and the system will still operate without the need to remove links now undefined. Similarly, a frame together with its attributes may be added and the system automatically takes it into account when links are generated.

The potential generality of this approach to knowledge representation is illustrated by its similarity to bit-mapped classifier approaches to the building of expert systems (Frey, 1986). These are pattern-recognition programs, in which a set of conditions is coded as a string of bits where each bit represents a feature or attribute that is present or absent (classifiers). Other bit strings can represent the relative importance of different features (classifier masks). This approach has been extended to sequential reasoning and machine learning (Holland, 1986) and bears many similarities to the representation method advocated here.

All hypertext systems devised to date suffer to a greater or lesser extent from the problems of navigation by the user and the risk of becoming 'lost in hyperspace'. These problems obviously become greater as the amount of material held increases. A system with fixed links has the advantage that in principle it should be possible to show maps of the local area or even provide overviews of the entire hyperspace. A system with dynamic links should be able to generate similar representations, but we have not demonstrated this point. One of the problems we foresee is that an attribute system defines a hyperspace of many dimensions, although admittedly degraded in our present implementations, and it may be difficult to represent this space on a computer screen. Techniques such as cluster analysis or principal components analysis may be be applicable here.

The generation of large hypertext systems is potentially fraught with problems. As more nodes are added so the number of links between them which need to be introduced, debugged, and adjusted increases at an even greater rate. If there are

N nodes, then there are N (N - 1) possible links between them, of which a fraction will be meaningful. The problem is one of order N2 and while not increasing exponentially with N , it will clearly become a serious problem to manage such complexity. As an example, Nelson (1988) in describing the structuring of links in the Xanadu hypertext project gives examples of document references containing 34 digits and although he does describe software which is intended to protect the user from such complexity, doubt must still remain about the ease of retrieving material from such a system. The intelligent system we propose may well require large sets of attributes to describe extensive amounts of material. However, it is likely that attributes may be redefined in 'local' areas, or have a structure imposed on them.

A further criticism of our suggested approach is the sheer scale of computation required in the simultaneous comparison of a probe with every frame in the database. This has not proved to be a problem in the small scale implementation of StrathTutor, but could well become prohibitive in the large hypertext systems we envisage. The nature of Hintzman's model is such that it is ideally structured for parallel computing, each trace required to react to the probe simultaneously, making a weighted contribution to the echo. It is likely that further progress with parallel computers will make our approach even more attractive.

References

Frey P W (1986) A bit-mapped classifier. *Byte*, 11 (11): 161-72.

Hardman L (1988) HyperTEXT '87 Workshop report. Scottish HCI Centre Internal Report, AMU 8824/01H.

Hintzman D L (1984) MINERVA 2: a simulation model of human memory. *Behaviour Research Methods, Instruments and Computers* 16 (2): 96-101.

Hintzman D L (1986) 'Schema abstraction' in a multiple-trace memory model. *Psychological Review* 93. pp 411-28.

Holland J (1986) Escaping brittleness: the possibilities of general purpose learning algorithms applied to parallel rule-based systems. In: *Machine Learning II.* Edited by Michalski R S, Carbonell J G and Mitchell T M. Morgan Kaufmann, Los Altos, CA.

Kohonen T (1987) *Content-addressable Memories.* Springer-Verlag, New York.

Mayes J T, Kibby M R and Watson H (1988) StrathTutor: the development and evaluation of a learning-by-browsing system on the Macintosh. *Computers and Education* 12. pp 221-9.

Nelson T H (1988) Managing immense storage. *Byte* 13 (1): 225-38.

Semon R (1923) *Mnemic psychology.* George Allen and Unwin, London.

Notes

[1] On secondment from the Department of Bioscience and Biotechnology.